The Caring Pastor

# THE CARING PASTOR

An Introduction
to Pastoral
Counseling in
the Local
Church

## Charles F. Kemp

ABINGDON PRESS / NASHVILLE

# THE CARING PASTOR

An Introduction to Pastoral Counseling in the Local Church

*Copyright © 1985 by Abingdon Press*

*This book is printed on acid-free paper.*

**Library of Congress Cataloging in Publication Data**

KEMP, CHARLES F., 1912–
  The caring pastor.
  1. Pastoral counseling.   I. Title
  BV4012.2.K438        1985        253.5        85-3994

**ISBN 0-687-04676-9**
(alk. paper)

Scripture quotations unless otherwise noted are from
the Revised Standard Version of the Bible, copyrighted
1946, 1952, 1971, © 1973, by the Division of Christian
Education of the National Council of the Churches of
Christ in the U.S.A., and used by permission.
Those noted KJV are from the King James Version.

Manufactured by the Parthenon Press at
Nashville, Tennessee, United States of America

TO

Dr. Charles Sanders
and
Dr. Albert Pennybacker

friends and colleagues

# Contents

# Preface

Several years ago when Norman Cousins visited Albert Schweitzer at his mission compound in Africa, the two men discussed great international problems. Cousins hoped to get Schweitzer to release some papers and to make a statement about nuclear testing. In the midst of their conversation, a nurse interrupted them and said a patient was having difficulty and she needed Dr. Schweitzer's instructions. After she had received the instructions, she apologized and left. Schweitzer turned to Cousins and said that in a world of great social issues, it is well to remember that individuals still have problems.

A Christian has been defined as "one who can read statistics with compassion." There are statistics enough. Every magazine, every newspaper, every newscast carries them. There are statistics about marriage and divorce, statistics about poverty and unemployment, statistics about mental illness and mental retardation, statistics about crime and delinquency, statistics about battered wives and abused children—the list goes on and on.

There are some things statistics do not show. There are figures on divorces granted, but there are no figures on those whose marriages are a constant source of strife and conflict. There are statistics on the number who are out of work. There are only guesses as to how many there are who do not enjoy their work or who just endure their work, wishing they were doing something else. There are statistics on the number admitted to mental hospitals, but there are no figures on the number of people who are seeing doctors but whose primary problems are emotional, or the number of people who are seeing psychologists and psychiatrists because they are mentally or emotionally disturbed. There are no statistics at all on the vast number of people in every community who are wandering in that "no man's land" that exists somewhere between happiness and discouragement, satisfaction and frustration, hope and despair, who are not seeing anyone about their problems but who could be helped if they could find someone who cared and could understand.

This book is about those people—great numbers of them—and how the working pastor can be of service to them. Many pastors are doing their best to minister to these people and would appreciate some help and guidance. Unfortunately, some pastors neglect such responsibilities because of the many other tasks they have to perform.

To paraphrase the words of Schweitzer, "in a world where sermons have to be prepared, committee meetings attended, where funds have to be raised and programs planned and promoted, it is well to remember that individuals still have problems and still need a ministry."

Many of these people seek the help of their pastor. They come with a wide variety of problems and concerns. They bring their hopes and their fears, their anxieties and their confusion, their concerns about themselves and their concerns about others; they may want to discuss their successes or their disappointments, their frustrations or their guilt, their decisions or their plans for the future. Every form of human perplexity, every emotion known to humankind may be brought to a pastor's door. Some problems may be simple, some may be complex, some may be transitory, some may be of long standing, but they are not the kinds of concerns that can be dealt with adequately by appointing a committee or even by preaching a sermon.

One of the highest compliments a parishioner can pay to a pastor is to say, not in words but in actions, "I trust you. I think you will understand. I think you care." Then the pastor is in truth "treading on holy ground." The whole future of that person or of that family may truly depend on how well the pastor can handle this situation. This is the challenge and the opportunity of parish pastoral counseling.

There is a tendency on the part of some people to think of counseling as the province of the specialist and to minimize, even to disparage, the parish pastor as counselor.

Of course, there is an important place for the counseling specialist. I have helped to train many of them and have served on the staff of one pastoral counseling center and as the consultant to another. I am well aware of the value of their services and the contribution they can make and shall speak of that in later pages.

However, the simple truth of the matter is that many people still go to their pastor for help. The parish pastor is in the front line of the mental health field whether he or she wants to be or not. In terms of numbers alone pastors of parish churches are doing more counseling than is being done by counseling specialists, whatever their setting or affiliation. For example, in the community where I live, there are two pastoral counseling centers and a half dozen or so pastoral counselors in private practice. Most of them are very busy and doing fine work. At the same time there are hundreds of churches, each with one or more pastors on their staffs. From my observation, the presence of these specialists has not diminished the number of people seeking help from their pastors. Furthermore, if all these pastors were to give up their counseling responsibilities and refer all their parishioners to the specialists, the number would be so overwhelming that the idea itself is preposterous.

In the state where I live there are several excellent pastoral counseling programs with various affiliations. Some are related to seminaries, some to councils of churches, some to groups of churches, and some have no definite church affiliation. The vast majority are in major metropolitan areas, while there are literally hundreds of towns and villages that have no pastoral counseling center and no specialists in pastoral counseling available and will not have in the foreseeable future. These people, too, have problems and concerns. It is the parish pastor who is the only one available to perform such ministry.

While my central focus is on "parish pastoral counseling," I am not ignoring the specialists. I hope that some of them will read these pages and will be made a little more aware of the place of the parish pastor, so that pastors and pastoral counselors might work in closer cooperation. Also, some of the topics I discuss here are just as applicable to the specialist as they are to the parish pastor.

I would be pleased if some lay persons might read these pages, also. Unfortunately many lay persons, even some leaders in church circles, are not aware of either the demands that counseling places on the pastors' time and energy or the opportunities for counseling services that a well-trained pastor presents to a congregation. I recall an incident when I was invited to preach a sermon in a local church. The man who introduced me was a prominent layman. He said something like this: "Our speaker this morning is a professor of pastoral care. I don't know what pastoral care is, but I assume it has something to do with the care of pastors." He was almost right.

Lay persons need to know that the pastor does some things other than what is done in public, such as preach sermons and attend committee meetings. Even more important, they need to know that the pastor is ready, willing, qualified, and able to help them as they face some of the deepest issues of life.

I especially hope that some theological students will also read this book and that it will help them to see the parish as a great field of service and parish pastoral counseling as a real challenge that will present them with many opportunities for a meaningful ministry.

Those familiar with the literature in the whole field of pastoral care and counseling will note some omissions. There is no discussion of such important areas of ministry as ministering to the sick, the sorrowing, the elderly, for example. I am well aware of the great significance of these areas of service, since they are just as important as some of the topics I have discussed. The reason I have not included them here is simply because they have been discussed so thoroughly in many volumes, and most pastors already see them as a part of their responsibility. I have chosen to include areas of service that are not as frequently discussed.

The original title of this book was *Parish Pastoral Counseling: Its Challenge and Its Opportunities,* a title that proved to be too cumbersome. *The Caring Pastor* is much better. However the ideas behind the original title still apply. (1) This book is directed to pastors who are serving in the parish. (2) My subject matter is pastoral counseling done in a local church setting. (3) This counseling presents the pastor with a great challenge and some tremendous opportunities, requiring a knowledge of many methods and techniques—both of which shall be pointed out. Most important is the attitude of the pastor. What people need today is someone who cares. This, then, is the real challenge and the opportunity shared by every pastor.

I have tried to keep references and quotations at a minimum and preserve a more conversational approach for easier reading. I would like to express my appreciation to Leah Flowers and Cherry Tackett, who prepared the manuscript after deciphering my very difficult-to-read handwriting.

# The Caring Pastor:

## A Rich Heritage

One time after I had made an address on the general subject of the pastoral ministry, a man asked me, "How long do you think this fad of pastoral counseling is going to last?"

I replied that it had lasted for many centuries and I assumed it would continue a while longer. His remark is symptomatic of a common misconception that pastoral counseling is something new, that it developed in the light of modern psychology. This is a complete misunderstanding of the facts. It is true that many things about pastoral counseling are new. There are new insights into human behavior, new techniques of counseling that have proved helpful, but pastoral counseling itself is very old. It is unfortunate that more pastors as well as people do not have a greater appreciation of their heritage.

I have long felt that the pastoral counseling movement needed a greater appreciation of its historical perspective for several reasons. A professor of mine used to say, "We never really know anything unless we know its history." Disraeli once said, "The greater our knowledge of what has been done, the greater will be our knowledge of what we ought to do." A knowledge of what has been done in the field of pastoral care can be very inspirational. Just to know of the faithful efforts of great preacher/pastors makes us aware of the tremendous things that can be accomplished when a pastor and a parishioner meet to share a common concern. It keeps us from getting cocky, for one thing. It remains to be seen whether, with all our sophisticated knowledge of psychological dynamics and counseling techniques, we will do any better than those of previous generations. They did it without training and without guidance, but they were effective. We have much to learn from them.

Pastoral counseling is one of those things that has a long past but a short history. Clear back in the Pentateuch, it says that Moses sat all day listening to the complaints of the people. That sounds rather modern in some respects. However, the complaints not only were dissatisfactions, but also were personal problems they brought to him as their religious leader. In fact, the burden became so great that he appointed others to help him with it.

In the Old Testament there were three groups of leaders—prophets, priests, and wise men. It was the wise men who gave counsel. The Book of Jeremiah states, "The law shall not perish from the priest, nor counsel from the wise, nor the word from the prophet" (18:18). The counsel they gave is summarized primarily in the book of Proverbs.

It had to do with family life, child rearing, controlling one's temper, and other day-to-day experiences.

The shepherd motif had its rise during the Exile when Ezekiel visited those in captivity down by the river Chebar and said, "I sat where they sat" (Ezek. 3:15 KJV). Today we would call that *empathy*. The shepherd theme is common in the Psalms. It found expression in the New Testament when Jesus looked on the crowds and was moved with compassion because they were like sheep without a shepherd. You can almost trace the life of Jesus in terms of the individuals to whom he ministered. In the book of John, Jesus refers to himself as the Good Shepherd (John 10:11).

A spirit of compassion continued in the early church and in the writings of Paul, which were primarily pastoral in purpose. There was much that was theological, to be sure, but his letters were personal, practical, and pastoral in intent. The first church officials were appointed for practical pastoral tasks.

This whole spirit of compassion was preserved through the Dark Ages by such men as Saint Francis, who cared for the hungry, the poor, the sick, in and around the village of Assisi, and thus shed the first light into the gloom of the Dark Ages. Saint Francis wasn't a pastoral counselor in any modern sense of the term, although many sought him for advice, but he kept alive the spirit of caring and concern that is the heart of the pastoral ministry.

This spirit of caring was continued by Protestant pastors such as Martin Luther, who is known chiefly as a theologian and a reformer, but his biographer said that at the height of the Reformation he never lost sight of the individual, for "no trouble seemed to him so trifling, no sorrow so insignificant, as to be unworthy of his ministry of comfort" (Nebe, *Luther as Spiritual Adviser,* Lutheran Publishing Society, 1894, p. 140). Luther, like many other pastors, had real insights into human needs and human nature. He once wrote, "When the heart is troubled and sorrowful, then follow weaknesses of the body. The diseases of the heart are the real diseases."

This spirit of pastoral concern was kept alive by lesser known pastors such as Richard Baxter in England, who was a great preacher—so good in fact that they had to enlarge his church in Kidderminster three times to get the people in. In his classical book *The Reformed Pastor* he said he had seen more results from one hour spent with a person "in straits" (as he described a troubled person) than from many sermons. He organized his time so that he could spend some time each year with each individual family and each person in it. There was no physician in Kidderminster, so he cared for the sick until the burden became so great he persuaded a "godly" physician to come and join him. There was no library available where books could be secured so he wrote books himself—some two hundred in all—and delivered them to his people, and we think we are busy? No pastor was ever more effective. He transformed the village of Kidderminster and said it was due primarily to his individual pastoral efforts.

This was also a part of the ministry of John Watson in Scotland, who lived by the motto, "Be kind, for everyone you meet is fighting a hard battle." These men took literally the words of Jesus, "Truly, I say to you, as you did it to one of the least of these my brethren, you did it to me" (Matt. 25:40).

Such pastoral concerns found expression in this country in such men as Phillips Brooks, who was recognized as probably the greatest preacher of his day, but his biographer said that his house was a refuge for all who were in trouble. They came at all hours of the day or night—all types and all ages—from all denominations and from all levels of society. Each person was met with sympathy and understanding. Each person was made to feel that his problem was the one thing of most concern to Phillips Brooks, as indeed at that moment it was. His friends urged him to seclude himself to protect his time and energy, but he refused, saying, "The man who wants to see me is the man I want to see."

These are but a few examples among many others not so well known who demonstrated the same concern and practiced a caring ministry. It is a great heritage of which we are a part. These pastors carried on a great ministry before there was any such thing as a course in pastoral care in a seminary, or a CPE (Clinical Pastoral Education) program, or even a book on pastoral counseling to guide them. They had no knowledge of psychology as such; the term hadn't even been coined yet, but they had a lot of common sense that was based on three important facts.

First, these pastors had many experiences with a wide range of people. Second, they made an intensive study of Scripture. The Bible is not a book on psychology or counseling techniques, but it is a literal storehouse of information about life. All the emotions known to humankind are found in the book of Psalms. The narrative accounts in both the Old and the New Testaments are filled with archetypes of human behavior that are true in every generation. Third, they spent much time in personal examination and self-evaluation. Many of them kept journals, a practice that only recently has been rediscovered as a source of insight and self-understanding. All this combined to give them a very practical background for dealing with people.

This is not to depreciate more recent learning. Entire sections shall be devoted to that in later chapters. It is to recognize that some things are very old, have been proven over the centuries, and should be neither overlooked nor discarded.

These pastors of a former generation have much to teach us. They were available. They gave of their time freely. They were faithful in their efforts. I used to tell my classes over and over again, "You are not called to be successful; you are called to be faithful." And faithfulness of effort does produce results.

We do not go to these pastors for instruction in counseling techniques, although some of them intuitively used methods that were effective. Phillips Brooks, for example, would sit for hours with people, just letting them talk. The fact is they knew nothing of such counseling techniques as shall be described later. Their procedures might be defined as trial and error, even floundering at times, but they tried, they were available, they were patient, they were kind, and they produced results.

Another factor should not be overlooked. They utilized spiritual resources, both in their own lives and in the lives of their people. Their pastoral efforts were deeply rooted in personal lives of meditation, prayer, and intercession, and they taught their people to pray and to trust.

Most important of all, they cared. The people knew it and this was a source of courage and strength. There are no modern sophisticated developments that take the place of such a spirit of love and trust. Such attitudes, then and now, are the basis of pastoral care and counseling.

## Modern Developments in Pastoral Counseling

About the turn of the century there came a dramatic change in the world's thinking. It dates from the work of Freud, Jung, and Adler in Vienna, and the efforts of William James and G. Stanley Hall in America. A new science was born—we entered the psychological age.

Now the world was different. It affected all areas that dealt with human behavior—medicine, education, social work—even the writing of history and biography would never be the same.

Pastors and the church were also influenced—especially in the areas of pastoral care and counseling. I intentionally included in the first part of this chapter names of pastors who preceded Freud. These great pastors had no benefit of psychological findings. To be sure many pastors were unaware of these new findings; others ignored them. Some opposed these new teachings, and some of these needed to be opposed. You couldn't reconcile early Watsonian behaviorism with the Christian faith, and Freud's *Future of an Illusion* needed to be challenged. However, there was a small group, characterized by such men as Leslie Weatherhead in London and Charles Holman at the University of Chicago, who began to study what the psychologists had to say and to make application to pastoral counseling.

These early pioneers were soon joined by such men as Seward Hiltner, Wayne Oates, and Carrol Wise, who refined the early discussions and put their thoughts in print.

This marked the first major step, the development of a body of literature on pastoral counseling as such. Prior to this, all a pastor had to read or study were the traditional books on what was called *practical theology*. These books covered the whole gamut of a pastor's liturgical, administrative, and pastoral responsibilities. They usually included a section on ministry to the sick and the bereaved, how to conduct weddings and baptisms, how to raise money and handle a board meeting. Hiltner, Oates, Wise, and others began to write books, entire books on pastoral counseling alone. I well remember how avidly we devoured them.

The next step was to incorporate pastoral counseling into the theological school curriculum. Courses in pastoral care and counseling found their place alongside other courses in the applied field such as homiletics and religious education. These courses were required just as were courses in theology, biblical studies, and church history. Very soon programs of Clinical Pastoral Education were accepted for credit toward a theological degree. This all had a real impact on theological education.

Out of all this there appeared a new group of specialists in the ministry. Just as the religious education movement had created a new specialty a generation before—directing religious education—so now the pastoral counseling movement created a new specialty—pastoral counseling. There had to be some specialists to teach the courses mentioned above. Very often this meant a pastor had to take a doctor's degree in counseling or psychology. There were no doctor's degrees in pastoral counseling as yet.

Another development was the training of institutional chaplains. There existed in this country thousands of people in mental and general hospitals, penal and correctional institutions, who received no ministry at all except in a few isolated situations. This was a vast mission field. One of the great services of the pastoral care movement was to fill this void. Now almost every institution has a resident chaplain—and some, two or three. They not only minister to the patients, but also provide supervised training for theological students.

The work of the chaplain is ecumenical in nature. Chaplains minister to all people, regardless of denominations. Their responsibilities are not limited to counseling, but it is a large part of what they do—for patients and for staff as well.

The next development was for pastors to do counseling outside the church—some of them did this counseling in private practice, like other therapists. Some worked in pastoral counseling centers. These centers began to appear in great numbers in the 1960s and 1970s. Some were associated with seminaries, some with councils of churches, some had no church connection of any sort. There is a regrettable tendency of some to separate themselves from the church and its heritage. Don Browning commented on this when he wrote, "Most of them practice their arts in special centers physically removed from the setting and life of the local chuch. What they do in their therapeutic sessions is widely acknowledged among themselves to be almost indistinguishable from what goes on in secular counseling" (Browning, The Moral Context of Pastoral Care, Westminster Press, 1976, p. 22).

All of this will no doubt continue. We will continue to study and learn from the psychotherapists. We will have new and hopefully better publications. Theological schools will continue to give pastoral care and counseling a prominent place in the curriculum. Training programs will be refined and improved. Specialization will probably increase. All of this is good—at least most of it is. We also feel it is extremely important that in the midst of all of these new developments and improvements we do not lose sight of the heritage of which we are a part. Pastors such as those mentioned in the first part of this chapter have much to say to us also.

In the midst of all the growth and improvement that is taking place, those of us who do pastoral counseling and pastoral care must preserve the four Cs that were so much a part of the faithful pastors' ministry throughout the long history of the church:

Caring

Concern

Compassion

Commitment

# Pastoral Counseling
# in the Local Church Setting

For years the only personal counseling that was done in America was done by the family doctor, the parish pastor, or some trusted friend. This sort of counseling was all there was for generations. Usually in the form of advice, such counseling was friendly, caring, and often very effective. I remember that when I began my ministry in the early 1930s, the only pastoral counseling done was by the pastor of a local church. There were no specialists in pastoral counseling in those days.

In the years since, two developments occurred that have greatly altered the whole counseling picture. The first was the emergence of the new psychology alluded to in the previous chapter. Professional organizations such as the American Psychological Association, the American Psychiatric Association, the American Personnel and Guidance

Association, and the Association of Marriage and Family Therapists included thousands of members, all specialists in some form of counseling.

All these developments put the local pastor in a totally different community from that which any previous generation of pastors had ever experienced. Just go back to Phillips Brooks' day and note the contrast. There were no psychiatrists in Boston; this was prior to the influence of Freud. There were no psychologists in Harvard; this was before William James became the first to hold such a position. There were no marriage counselors or family service associations; these are twentieth-century developments. Phillips Brooks and his fellow pastors did what counseling was done, or it didn't get done.

Now all of this is changed. If one would check the yellow pages in Boston today, one would find literally hundreds of psychologists, psychiatrists, family therapists, and social service agencies of many types and descriptions. The same would be true in any city. This is good for several obvious reasons. For one thing, it means more people are getting help. It also means there are now many people specially trained to perform services and to meet needs that the pastor is not trained to meet. This gives the pastor a source of referral for special problems and leaves the pastor free to function as a pastor. I used to tell my classes, "Never attempt to do what someone else can do better."

This proliferation of counselors has been so great that some have raised the question, "Is there still a place for the pastor in the counseling field?" It has been said, "The analyst's couch has replaced the confessional; the marriage therapist is replacing the pastoral counselor."

Even some pastors may doubt their place and tend to feel somewhat inferior to those in the other professions who have such extended training and specialized skills. Paul Pruyser, a psychologist at the Menninger Foundation, said it was his observation, in watching pastors as they worked alongside psychiatrists, psychologists, and social workers at the Menninger Clinic, that they tended to downgrade themselves and often acted like amateurs in the midst of professionals. Dr. Pruyser further stated that this ought not to be. The pastor is a professional, too, with special training and with the availability of spiritual resources that have been proven over the centuries as means of health and strength.

In spite of this twentieth-century phenomenon, the fact remains that many people still think of their pastor in a time of need. One study quoted widely a few years ago, *The Nation Views Its Mental Health,* revealed that in time of stress 42 percent of the American people think first of all of their pastor. This is in contrast to 26 percent who thought first of their doctor; the remaining 32 percent were divided between all the other helping professions.

The second development, which came a bit later, was the emergence of the specialists in pastoral counseling, also referred to in the previous chapter, plus the appearance of pastoral counseling centers and pastors who began to engage in the "private practice" of pastoral counseling, quite separate from a church. Most of these men and women had the same general theological training as the parish pastor, plus they usually had extended training in CPE and a few had completed Ph.D. degrees in psychology in addition to their theological training. Some people who a generation ago would have sought out their pastor were now going to pastoral counseling centers.

Again this development raised the same question. Is there a place for pastoral counseling by pastors in the local church when there are specialists in pastoral counseling available? Some pastors admitted feelings of inadequacy as they compared themselves with these new specialists in the ministry.

Again the answer is a decided yes. There *is* a place for pastoral counseling in the local church. If the study referred to above were to be repeated today, I am quite sure the findings would be very similar. The majority of people would still say they think first of their pastor, not a specialist, either secular or pastoral.

The needs are so great and the numbers of people seeking help are so large that there is plenty to be done by both parish pastors and pastoral counseling specialists.

A recent development is the adding of counseling specialists to the professional staff of churches. This is very similar to what took place a generation ago when ministers of education were added to church staffs. Whether pastoral counselors will be as common on church staffs in the future as directors of religious education are now remains to be seen. This is obviously limited to larger churches, and larger churches, like pastoral counseling centers, are located primarily in urban communities. In smaller communities and smaller churches, the parish pastor is going to be the counselor if there is one.

Let's make one point perfectly clear. The parish pastor and the pastoral counseling specialist should not be in competition with each other in any way. Their relationship should be one of mutual understanding and cooperation. Parish pastors on occasion should refer to pastoral counselors and vice versa. Each has a unique role to play and contributions to make.

The pastoral counseling specialist usually devotes full time to counseling and does not need to work his or her counseling hours in between sermon preparation and committee meetings. In most cases these specialists have had extended, supervised pastoral education, which enables them to deal with some situations a parish pastor might not want to attempt. In such cases the pastoral counseling specialist is a good source of referral.

I do not mean to imply that the parish pastor should avoid all difficult or long-term situations. Many parish pastors have had excellent training in counseling and are as qualified as anyone else. Their chief limitation is one of time. In some situations, the fact that the counselor is the pastor of a church is a distinct advantage.

A question frequently asked is, "How does pastoral counseling differ from general or secular counseling?" In many respects they are very similar. Listening, for example, is a primary method used by pastors and psychotherapists alike. One who listens with empathy and understanding provides a service, whether done by a pastor or a psychologist. The same is true of interpretation, reassurance, and other procedures. But there are some differences. The most obvious difference lies in the training. Most professionals see people from the perspective of their training. Physicians see them in terms of their physical symptoms and physical needs. More and more physicians are coming to recognize that physical ills cannot be separated from emotional and mental attitudes, but by and large, they are trained to be aware of physical ills, which is as it should be. The psychiatrist is specially trained to diagnose and treat mental and emotional ills. The psychologist sees people in terms of conditioned responses, mental abilities, or emotional reactions, depending upon the particular school of psychotherapy in which the psychologist was trained. The pastor sees people theologically and biblically. That is the way the pastor was trained. Pastors see persons as children of God, the objects of God's love, created in his image. This makes a significant difference in pastors' attitudes toward troubled persons and in the approach they take to meeting their needs.

The different professionals also differ in the skills they can utilize. The physician is trained in prescribing medication and performing surgery. The psychologist is trained in administering and interpreting psychological tests and in counseling techniques. The pastor is trained in counseling, too, but also in the use of spiritual disciplines, in dealing with life's meanings and values, in the power of faith and love.

The different professionals also differ in their goals and objectives. The doctor's goal is to alleviate pain and restore health. The psychologist's goal is to help attain emotional adjustment and resolve neuroses. The pastor, too, hopes that health can be restored and that anxiety can be reduced, but beyond this, the pastor thinks in terms of grace, forgiveness, redemption, and salvation. Such matters are of profound importance both to pastors and to the people with whom a pastor works.

There are other areas in which the pastor of a local church differs even from the specialist in pastoral counseling.

The setting itself makes a difference. There have been research studies that demonstrate people enter a church building with different attitudes from those with which they go to a hospital, a clinic, a school, a social agency, or an office building (see Seward Hiltner and Lowell Colston, *The Context of Pastoral Counseling,* Abingdon Press, 1961).

Another difference in the various specialists is the symbolic role each profession carries. The physician, the psychiatrist, the psychologist, the social worker, the pastor—all have symbolic roles. These roles can be either negative or positive in their influence. The attitudes people have toward a pastor are different from the attitudes they have toward any other professional. It all depends on their previous experience with pastors, which can make it easier for some to come to a pastor and more difficult for others. Usually, however, it is a positive influence. The pastor represents far more than his or her own personality. The pastor represents the fellowship of the church, the whole historic tradition of the Christian faith. In a very real sense, the pastor represents God.

The pastor also has a relationship with the ones he or she counsels that is different from that of other professionals. The pastor participates in a continuing relationship that begins before the specific problem occurs and continues after the counseling is discontinued. The relationship of other professionals to someone they counsel begins with the occurrence of the difficulty; they have no previous background knowledge of the person. Their relationship is terminated when the counseling is terminated. They have no means of knowing how the person is progressing after the counseling is over. The pastor has a background to begin with and knows when relapses occur and whether counseling should be activated again. This is a distinct advantage.

The pastor also can initiate a relationship. Most other professionals cannot. If a pastor becomes aware that a need is present, the pastor can call in the home or at the office. The pastoral call has centuries of tradition behind it. Pastoral calling is not as popular as it once was for many reasons, but it is still an accepted part of a pastor's role. A pastoral call may meet a specific need, such as sickness or trouble, or it may be just to get acquainted, but even these calls sometimes lead to counseling which might not have occurred at all except that the pastor was present and showed concern.

Sometimes there are situations where a pastor cannot call. There are seldom situations where the pastor cannot use the telephone. Just a five- or ten-minute conversation may provide a lot of encouragement and support. If one can't call or phone, there is always the mail.

Henri Nouwen in *The Genesee Diary* said, "It remains remarkable how little is said and written about letter writing as an important form of ministry. A good letter can change the day for someone in pain, can chase away feelings of resentment, can create a smile and bring joy to the heart" (Doubleday, 1976, p. 71).

Strangely enough, we cannot find anything in the literature on pastoral counseling that refers to letter writing as a technique. Much can be done to supplement counseling by the use of the mail. In one sense this is a form of pastoral conversation, but is written instead.

Most of the New Testament is of this type. The Pauline epistles are primarily pastoral in nature. They have been analyzed critically, historically, theologically, but they were written pastorally. They were written to meet the personal, practical, religious needs of individuals and congregations.

Several were written at the request of individuals or groups who had written or sent messengers to seek Paul's advice (or counsel). These letters were informal in nature, often highly personal, not written with any thought of scholarly examination or with any literary ambition at all. Their purpose, tone, content, and nature were pastoral.

Pastors for generations have written to offer guidance and help, often with real, lasting results. Phillips Brooks almost made an art of it. He studied how to write letters of encouragement and consolation as others studied their sermons. Horace Bushnell carried on a voluminous correspondence with people who were in trouble. *The Life and Letters of Horace Bushnell,* written by his daughter, Mary A. Cheney, includes many of these letters. There are letters to those who were sick and letters to those in trouble. There is one account of a correspondence carried on for years with a person in another city whom Bushnell had never met, who wrote him asking for the secret of "strength and peace."

In addition to the specific counsel, guidance, encouragement, or support that a pastor can give in a letter, there are two other values that such a process provides. One, when people receive a letter, they can read it and reread it until it becomes incorporated into their own thoughts. They may forget what is said in a counseling hour, but they can preserve a letter and refer to it repeatedly.

Also, writing can do the counselee a lot of good. Expressing oneself on paper can reduce tension and often lead to insights just as talking does. It is a useful procedure to ask people to write out their thoughts and feelings, to put them on paper, look at them again so that they will gain a new understanding of their situation. When this procedure is coupled with an understanding reply, it can have great therapeutic value.

It also can be helpful for a pastor to write summary letters to counselees. Such letters outline the situation as the pastor sees it, reinforce areas of growth, make suggestions for further growth. A lot of the value lies in the fact that the pastor took the time to do it, and that in itself assures the person that someone cares. Again, the pastoral role comes into play. It is not the usual practice for professionals to carry on such correspondence with their clients, but a pastor can do so. Pastors have been writing pastoral letters for centuries.

This is an area of pastoral counseling that has been largely neglected. A lot has been written about pastoral calling and counseling, but very little has been written about pastoral correspondence.

There are some areas of life where the pastor is considered to be the specialist. This is especially true of religious, theological, or existential questions. These questions may deal with religious belief, doubt, prayer, sin, and guilt, or any matter that has to do with life's meaning and value. There may be questions about religious culture and traditions, such as the meaning of church membership, baptism, the Lord's Supper, denominational differences, or any other matter pertaining to religious practices. Or questions may have to do with life's ultimate loyalties and commitments—the heart of religion.

There are other areas of experience where the pastor, because of the pastoral role, is in a unique position to help. Premarital counseling and guidance is one example. The pastor is the one who conducts the wedding; the pastor is the one who is expected to provide premarital guidance and instruction. This is also true of marriage and family life. The pastor not only conducts weddings and preaches on love and understanding, but also identifies with the home and family in many ways. The pastor shares both the joys and the sorrows of life with families, and in many ways expresses interest and concern. When a specific problem arises, it is quite natural that the members of the family turn to one they know and trust. They know the pastor is concerned about them, their children, their elderly parents, or whoever may be involved. (A whole chapter will be devoted to this subject later.) The only limitations of the pastor as a marriage and family counselor are time and training.

Another factor, which separates the pastor from other counselors, is that the pastor is more than a counselor. The pastor also performs many other functions, some of which have a direct or indirect relationship to counseling. The pastor also preaches, teaches frequently, conducts worship, and administers. Mental health workers recognize the importance of support groups. They speak of the value of "belonging" to something worthwhile. They recognize the therapeutic value of being part of a group where one is accepted and loved. The pastor has a natural support group in the congregation. Granted, not all churches provide the redemptive community that they should, yet certain elements of such a community are usually there, and the possibilities are always there. One of the real therapeutic values of the church is the fact that it is not a therapy group. It is a fellowship of worship, service, and faith, which is very therapeutic.

Many things provide healing for the mind and spirit, none more than doing something for someone else or rendering a service to a cause known to be worthwhile. Paul Pruyser, the psychologist mentioned earlier, speaking of the unique opportunities of the clergy, said, "Perhaps the judicious issuing of tasks, the imposition of chores and nudging clients on toward acts of charity are some of the special theological resources of pastoral care" ("The Use and Neglect of Pastoral Resources," *Pastoral Psychology*, 1971, p. 171).

The usual emphasis on service is that there are causes and individuals that need to be served. That is still valid and much needed. We are speaking here of another value of service—that is, the value that comes to the one who serves. In helping people find tasks of service, we also help them gain freedom from their worries and concerns, and they often gain a sense of satisfaction and fulfillment they would not find in any other way.

Theologically speaking, we can hardly be said to be spiritually healthy until we think more of others than of ourselves. Many people need to forget themselves as much as they need to analyze themselves. This is not to ignore the importance of facing personal concerns or of dealing with personal problems. This must be done. It is simply to recognize that the *abundant life* (to use the New Testament term) or *self-actualization* (to use the psychological term) comes not only by understanding ourselves but by giving ourselves.

Some are fortunate enough to find such opportunities in their vocations. Many must find such avenues of service outside their occupations. It need not be something dramatic or exciting. It may be quite simple—writing a letter, doing volunteer work, serving on a committee in the church, helping a friend.

The pastor, in making such suggestions, must be specific and realistic. Individual differences of interest, ability, and opportunity must be taken into account. Not all people want to or should serve in the same way. That is biblical, too. "Now there are varieties of gifts, but the same Spirit; and there are varieties of service, but the same Lord; and there are varieties of working, but it is the same God" (I Cor. 12:4-6). The pastor should be as careful in helping people find the right field of service as the vocational counselor is careful in helping people find the right career. This is real pastoral administration.

The fact is that biblically, all people are called to serve. Psychologically, all people need to serve. Personal concerns seem smaller when our attention is focused on others or on a worthwhile cause. New strength is discovered when it is called out to meet a real need. Life has a deeper meaning when it is invested in causes outside ourselves.

It is only fair to recognize that many of these things listed as advantages can be disadvantages as well. Some people do not feel comfortable going into a church building or talking to a member of the clergy. They fear he or she will be judgmental, moralistic, or will not understand. The fact that they will have a continuing relationship with the pastor may make it difficult for some to discuss their personal feelings or behavior. If they have been friends with the pastor, it may be difficult for them to confess their anger or their guilt. For such persons, the anonymity of a specialist's office may be preferable.

In summary, let us say that the presence of specialists, both secular and pastoral, is good, and their numbers will no doubt increase—for that we should be grateful. At the same time, this in no way diminishes the need for or the importance of pastoral counseling in the parish church. People will still seek their pastor for help, which is as it should be. That is what the pastor is there for. Nothing will or should replace this. There is something sacred about those occasions when a pastor sits down with an individual or a family, a part of his or her congregation or, as Richard Baxter would put it, a part of the "flock." Then the pastor is in the counseling arena whether he or she wants to be or not.

I have heard of a book club that was evaluating its services through its members. A question about one club selection was asked, "Have you read this book?" One respondent said, "Not personally."

Some things can only be done personally. They can't be done by appointing a committee, or preaching a sermon, or even by referral. Some things a pastor has to deal with personally. There will always be a place for this deep personal, one-to-one relationship as long as the church continues.

The pastor should never feel that pastoral counseling is of secondary importance to the work of anyone else. At times a referral may be indicated, but even then the pastor should remember that the pastor, too, is a specialist, but more than this, the pastor is a servant, who serves in the name of him who spoke to crowds but also ministered to people one by one, and who said, "As you did it to one of the least of these, my brethren, you did it to me" (Matt. 25:40).

Pastoral counseling in a local church is a real privilege and a great opportunity.

# Learning from the Psychologists:

## Understanding Human Behavior

For several years in a seminary I taught a course entitled "Schools of Psychotherapy." The course description explained that the purpose of the class was to explore what these various schools of thought had to contribute to the work of the pastor and the pastor's understanding of the parishioners in the congregation. It was a rewarding but frustrating course to teach—rewarding because it provided so many insights that helped me to better understand the people I was counseling, frustrating because the field was so vast and in such a constant state of flux that I realized I could never really complete the course in the time allotted and that I would have to rework it at least every two years to keep up with the new developments.

In surveying the whole field of psychotherapy, I became aware that in some ways, there were many similarities to the church, although some of my psychologist friends would disagree. For example:

— The psychologists have their prophetic, innovative leaders. The church has its outstanding leaders.
— The psychologists have their training centers; they call them graduate schools. The church has training centers; they call them theological schools.
— The psychologists have requirements for practicing their profession; they call it certification. The church has requirements for practicing ministry; they call it ordination.
— The psychologists have their sacred literature. The church has its sacred literature and authoritative writing.
— The psychologists have professional journals; the church has professional journals.
— The psychologists have developed their own psychological language; the church has developed its own theological vocabulary.

The pastoral counselor has much to learn from the psychotherapists. Primarily, what he or she has to learn centers in two fields: (1) personality theory, which helps the pastor understand his or her parishioners, and (2) counseling methods and techniques, which give practical suggestions in dealing with specific situations. I will discuss the first in this chapter and the second in the next. Both these areas are so vast that I feel like the young student who decided he would write a book. He took his manuscript to one of his professors and said, "This is only the first chapter, in which I explain the universe."

To attempt to discuss schools of psychotherapy in one chapter borders on the ridiculous. If I couldn't complete it in a year's lectures, how can I condense it into one chapter? Obviously I can only touch on the high spots and leave it to the reader to fill in the gaps. I have chosen to do it by using personalities and will do it more or less chronologically.

I am not attempting to cover the whole range of any person's thought or of any school's complexities. I am only discussing those areas that seem to me to have a direct bearing on pastoral counseling. I recognize that this is highly subjective. Others might go to the same school, or the same persons, and find different things to emphasize.

If we are going to look at schools of psychotherapy historically, we have to begin with Sigmund Freud and psychoanalysis. Psychoanalysis challenged the thinking of the pastor at several points. First of all, it made pastors aware of the reality of the unconscious. Human nature was seen as much more complex than pastors had once realized. There were not only the conscious words that could be heard and behavior that could be observed but there were also unconscious, or subconscious, forces operating below the surface. These forces manifested themselves in many ways, in dreams, in slips of the tongue, in physical symptoms, and in defense mechanisms.

A *defense mechanism* is an unconscious method by which we defend ourselves against anxiety, feelings of guilt or inadequacy. These methods can be observed in every congregation. Some of the most common are projection, rationalization, denial, displacement, and repression.

*Projection* is the way we protect ourselves from embarrassment or guilt by projecting onto others thoughts, feelings, or desires that are unacceptable to the self. So the parishioner blames others for failure at a task, or reduces his or her own guilt by saying it was someone else's fault. Adam said, "The woman gave me the fruit." Eve said, "The snake made me eat the apple."

*Rationalization* occurs all the time. This is how we ascribe to ourselves other motives, thoughts, or feelings than the ones that really exist. Aesop knew this long before Freud. Because the fox couldn't reach the grapes, he said they were sour. Because the candidate for office in the church is defeated, he says he didn't want the job anyway.

*Denial* is the refusal to admit consciously certain thoughts, feelings, or wishes that are socially or personally unacceptable. As Shakespeare put it in one of his plays, "The lady doth protest too much, methinks."

*Displacement* is the redirection of energy from the original object to a more acceptable substitute object. A man may be bawled out by his boss. When he goes home, he takes out his anger on his wife and child. The child goes out and kicks the cat. The word *scapegoat* goes clear back to Leviticus.

All this is done unconsciously. There are also repressed emotions. Perhaps *repression* is the most common defense mechanism of all. It is defined as the involuntary banishment of unacceptable ideas or impulses into the unconscious. Every pastor sees people who are repressing anger, guilt, doubt—almost every day.

Another of Freud's concepts that has significance for the pastor is his explanation of the *transference* phenomenon. Freud pointed out that patients (parishioners) transferred to the therapist (pastor) unconscious feelings of anger, guilt, or love that they felt for significant others in earlier life. These feelings could be negative or positive, indifferent or erotic. The parishioner (patient) may see the pastor (therapist) as he or she really is—a minister who is hopefully kind and understanding and is willing to help. Or the parishioner unconsciously may see the pastor as mother, father, judge, enemy, lover, or in various other roles as the case may be. This transference may lead to much confusion and, on occasion, to misunderstanding and embarrassment.

The pastor also has unconscious needs, desires, feelings, and may project these onto the parishioner. This is *counter-transference.* This occurs in all interpersonal relationships but is more likely to occur in pastoral care and counseling than in any other aspect of the pastor's task because of the emotions that are involved. In counseling with pastors, many of the problems that occur are a result of the pastor's failure to be aware of the transference or counter-transference that is taking place.

There are many other psychoanalytic concepts, too numerous to mention here.

One of Freud's best known pupils was a young Jewish physician named Alfred Adler. Adler and Freud split over Freud's pansexuality theory, and when Freud demanded complete acceptance of his views, Adler and several others withdrew and formed a rival organization called Individual Psychology.

Adler is best known for his emphasis on inferiority feelings. "I am the legitimate father of the inferiority complex," he once claimed. This, not repressed sex, is the cause of the neurosis. Adler also claimed that feelings of inadequacy or inferiority are universal, "To be human is to feel inadequate."

These feelings of inferiority often result in *compensations,* a striving for superiority, a desire to excel, the attempt to surmount others. The way a person works out these feelings of inadequacy, these strivings for superiority, results in a life-style.

Everyone has a life-style. It is pretty well formulated in childhood and is modified by all succeeding experiences. This life-style can be healthy or unhealthy, neurotic or wholesome. It is not in exploring the unconscious that we discover a person's needs but in analyzing the life-style. The only healthy life-style is one that culminates in "social interest." But Adler also contended that every person has a "creative self." This is the human capacity to choose one's life-style.

Adler made pastors aware of the ubiquity of feelings of inadequacy. If he is right, inadequacy is a problem for every member of the congregation. Also, everyone has a life-style. This, too, is a concern of the church. The Christian life is a life-style.

Another of Freud's pupils who also split off to form his own school was Carl Jung, perhaps the most brilliant of them all and certainly the most difficult to understand. Some authorities claim that even Jung didn't understand Jung.

He was the son of a clergyman and retained an interest in things religious all his life. In fact, he saw a great place for religion and attracted the attention of many clergy primarily because of a statement in his book *Modern Man in Search of a Soul* (Harcourt, Brace, & Co., 1933).

> Among all my patients in the second half of life—that is to say, over thirty-five—there has not been one whose problem in the last resort was not that of finding a religious outlook on life. It is safe to say that every one of them fell ill because he had lost that which the living religions of every

age have given to their followers, and none of them has been really healed who did not regain his religious outlook.

In 1921 Jung wrote *Psychological Types*. In this book he presented the concept of the extrovert and the introvert, which should have had a larger influence on the clergy than it has. Congregations are made up of people—some of whose interests are external, active, social; others are more introverted, internal, introspective. Many are in between.

There is no good or bad about this. It is just that people are different. The extrovert is going to be interested in fellowship groups, action projects, doing a lot of things. The introvert is going to be interested in prayer study groups, reading, and meditation. This concept creates problems when the pastor appoints an introvert as chairperson of the social action committee and an extrovert as chairperson of the fellowship of prayer. It also makes a difference in counseling procedures. The extrovert will respond to action, behavior-oriented suggestions. The introvert will respond more to insight-oriented approaches, to reading between sessions and suggestions for meditation.

The biggest difference between Jung and Freud is their concept of the unconscious. For Freud, the unconscious is filled with devils, the source of most of our difficulty and pain. For Jung, the unconscious is also the source of good, the seat of creativity and inspiration.

The two concepts that are unique to Jung are his belief in a collective unconscious and archetypes. Jung felt that the unconscious included not only one's own repressed experiences but the accumulated deposits of the race. This includes all races and all generations. It is an accumulation of predispositions and potentialities. There are common elements that all people, all races, all cultures, all generations, share.

Some common archetypes are: the hero, the king, the demon, the grand old man. These archetypes are the greatest influence in a person's life.

The Bible is full of archetypes. Goliath is an archetype—the evil giant who must be destroyed. Abraham—the patriarch—is an archetype. Most churches have a patriarch in the congregation. Moses—the wise old man—is an archetype. Samuel—the kingmaker—is an archetype. Mary Magdalene—the sinner who was converted—is an archetype. The self-righteous Pharisee is also an archetype—often seen among some church members. Paul/Saul is an archetype of the inner struggle that all people share—"For I do not do the good I want, but the evil I do not want is what I do" (Rom. 7:19). How many times have I heard the statement, "I don't know why I do these things."

Whether or not Jung's concepts are a contribution to our thoughts about persons depends on whether or not we accept the idea of the collective unconscious and archetypes.

All these men were the so-called depth psychologists. They had a background of medicine. Their insights came primarily from the consulting room, deep introspection, and self-analysis. Both Freud and Jung analyzed themselves thirty minutes a day. They were men of genius, dependent primarily on their own insights and the dialogue, sometimes bitter, which took place between them.

Then another group appeared in the psychotherapeutic field, not psychiatrists but psychologists. The background of their work was not the consulting room but the research lab. Their setting was not the hospital but the campus.

One of the first psychologists to gain national attention was E. G. Williamson of the University of Minnesota. Williamson and his colleagues were experimenting with a theory, a system designed to help university students. Their major concern was career planning, vocational choice. This was sometimes called the Minnesota Point of View, sometimes Clinical Counseling, but a more accurate definition is the Trait Factor Theory. They felt that everyone is a combination of certain traits, factors, aptitudes, abilities, interests, and personality traits, all of which could be measured, diagnosed, and predictions made as to what could be expected academically and vocationally. This theory had very little influence on pastoral counseling. Public school counseling, yes—pastoral counseling, no. We shall return to this in chapter 6 when we discuss the Vocational Guidance Movement.

In the midst of all this there came a new emphasis, which was in part a revolt against psychoanalysis and the clinical counseling of the day. It was led by Carl Rogers, who had studied for the ministry but changed to psychology, feeling the ministry would be too confining.

He had developed some ideas that were directly counter to Freud's analysis and Williamson's diagnosis. He felt both were a violation of personality and actually counterproductive to the counseling process. He felt that only the individual has the understanding of his or her own problem and also the resources for its solution.

In the 1940s Rogers made public his ideas in a book called *Counseling and Psychotherapy*. In this book he used an unfortunate term, *nondirective counseling*. Later in another book he called it *client-centered* therapy, although many still continue to use the former term.

His thesis was that the counseling process was centered in the client, not the counselor. It depended on an understanding of two key terms, *acceptance* and *reflection of feelings.* The whole process consisted of creating a climate of unconditional acceptance and reflecting back to the client the feelings that were being expressed.

This client-centered therapy led to self-understanding, self-acceptance, to more authentic feelings and behavior. Pastors flocked to this point of view in great numbers. I still recall the optimism it brought to those of us in the counseling field. It seemed like a good solution to both the long, involved process of psychoanalysis and the mechanical testing procedures of Williamson. For a decade or so, most pastoral counseling books were heavily influenced by Rogerian principles—and not without benefit.

Such principles did provide some very valuable insights to the pastor. Rogers stressed his conviction that all individuals have within themselves a drive toward maturity, self-actualization, and congruence. This drive didn't have to be imparted from the outside. It was simply there, just as present as the healing forces within the body. What needed to be done was to release it—to let it actualize itself.

Another value for the clergy was Rogers' emphasis on accepting every person as a person of unconditional worth. At this point he challenged the clergy at their own game. The clergy had been preaching about lost sheep, hating the sin but loving the sinner, for years. They had been talking theologically about a God who accepts the unacceptable. Now Rogers talked about actually doing this with real people.

Unconditional acceptance is not as easy as some thought. It takes a lot of understanding, empathy, imagination, patience, and a few other virtues, but it is all-important. To accept those who disagree with us, those who oppose us, those whose behavior is offensive, even repulsive, as persons of unconditional worth is not easy. Preaching a sermon on the prodigal son is a lot simpler than accepting a few prodigals.

Client-centered therapy made a real contribution to pastoral counseling, but as time went by we found that it had limitations in some settings. Also, it was contrary to a pastor's role just to reflect feelings and avoid all forms of interpretation and confrontation.

There appeared other schools, which were, in the main protests, or refinements of earlier emphases. The whole school of behavior modification or *learning theory* had a much greater influence on clinical counseling than it did on pastoral counseling. Learning theory had a background of behaviorism and went back not to Freud but to Pavlov. One of the early pioneers was Josef Wolpe, who became dissatisfied with his psychoanalytic training and was searching for a new approach.

The learning theorists based their whole theory on the premise that all behavior is learned behavior. That means *all* behavior: good behavior and bad behavior, healthy behavior and unhealthy behavior, the behavior of sinners, the behavior of saints. The learning theorists were interested in modifying behavior; they were not interested in insight.

Religion has always been concerned about behavior and behavior change. Preachers for generations have been warning from the pulpit that some forms of behavior are wrong and that other forms of behavior are right. The Ten Commandments deal primarily with behavior. The book of Proverbs, the exhortations of the prophets, instruct us on how to behave. The New Testament does not include as many legal requirements, but there are many admonitions to be kind, to feed the hungry, to treat other people the way you want to be treated. All this has to do with behavior.

Behavioral counseling is based on certain major premises. One we have already stated. All behavior is learned. It has been conditioned and reinforced over a long period of time. A second premise is that what has been learned can be unlearned. This is called *extinction*. The third is that good, better, more appropriate behavior can be learned and developed. This is done through *reinforcement*. A large number of techniques have been developed, all of which are designed to change behavior. Some of them shall be discussed in the next chapter.

Whereas pastors have been dealing with behavior for centuries, the learning theorists contend that the pastors' work in this area has been ineffective because it has not been done scientifically and systematically. There can be no doubt that much of the behavior the pastor sees is learned. Finding ways to eliminate bad behavior and develop good behavior is one of the pastor's primary tasks. The popularity of other schools of psychotherapy, which emphasize thoughts and feelings, has caused some pastoral counselors to ignore or avoid dealing with behavior as such. The contention of such schools is that if the thoughts and feelings are correct, then the behavior will take care of itself. The behavioral counselors, on the contrary, contend that if the behavior can be corrected, then the thoughts and feelings will improve. The parish pastor is concerned about both.

There also appeared several charismatic figures in the world of psychology who attracted enough followers that their ideas could be rightfully called a school. These figures usually stressed one idea or theme, often to the exclusion of most others. Several clergy were numbered in their followers. Without the space to discuss them in detail, all I can do is note who they are, what school they represent, and their central theme or point of view.

William Glaser was another psychoanalyst who became frustrated with his practice and began looking for new solutions. He came into prominence when he was the psychiatric consultant for the Ventura School for Girls in California. He found that the only method that proved effective with them was to confront them with their responsibility. He would permit no evasions. They could rationalize, evade, shift the blame—but he would always come back, "But who did the shoplifting?" The key question was, "What is the most responsible thing you can do?"

*Responsibility* is the key word. In fact, Glaser would not use the term *mental illness* but called it *irresponsible behavior*. He felt the most therapeutic thing you could do for a person was to insist on responsible behavior. He published his findings in a book called *Reality Therapy.* Many pastors read this book. In fact Glaser told me in a private conversation that he had a better response from pastors than he did from psychiatrists.

Viktor Frankl was also trained in the psychoanalytic tradition. He had shown great promise, had written a manuscript that he felt would establish him in his profession. Then came the war. He was a Jew in a Nazi country. His experience in a concentration camp is too familiar to be repeated here. Suffice it to say that out of this experience, plus his work with patients after his release, he was led to the position that the neuroses of the twentieth century are not caused by repressed sex, not by feelings of inadequacy, but by a lack of meaning. He called this position *logotherapy*. His autobiographical book, *The Search for Meaning,* was widely ready by the clergy. In a more recent publication, *The Unheard Cry for Meaning,* Frankl says, "It is precisely this will to meaning that remains unfulfilled by today's society—and disregarded by today's psychology" (Simon & Schuster, 1978, p. 29).

Another group has attracted rather wide attention—the cognitive therapists such as Aaron Beck and David Burns. This group also includes the thinking of Albert Ellis, Maxie Maltsby, and Paul Hauck, who call their approach *rational emotive therapy* (RET). The cognitive therapists all agree that thoughts determine feelings. Two people may experience the same event—one becomes angry, the other may be amused; two people may experience a similar event—one becomes anxious, the other remains undisturbed. The difference is not in the event but in what the different people thought about it.

The cognitive therapists agree that some very common irrational ideas that are characteristic of our culture cause people to become upset or disturbed. One of these faulty ideas that causes a lot of people concern is the idea that we should be liked or loved by almost every other person in our lives. If we are disliked or disapproved of, we think it awful. Many young pastors leave seminary with high ideals and lofty purposes. They go to their first churches and find that not everyone shares their ideas or their enthusiasm. Some may be openly critical. This can be most discouraging.

Actually, it should be expected. Religious leaders have had to face apathy, opposition, and criticism ever since Paul served his churches in the New Testament.

Another unrealistic idea is that we should never make mistakes, that we should be successful in everything we undertake. To make mistakes, to be less than perfect, is terrible. A third unrealistic idea is that other people should act the way we want them to act, that things should be the way we want them to be. If we start with these assumptions, then the results are going to be disturbing because this just isn't the way it is. Burns and Beck call these unrealistic ideas cognitive distortions. Ellis and Maltsby call them irrational self-talk.

The purpose of therapy is to help persons think rationally, free of all cognitive distortions. Helping persons to think rationally is also a goal of pastoral counseling. Both in pastoral counseling and in church administration, the pastor sees people with unrealistic expectations of perfection, thinking emotionally rather than realistically, overreacting to situations unnecessarily. If the pastor can help them think rationally, realistically, and healthily he or she has performed a real service.

There are many other schools too numerous to mention. In fact, clear back in 1974, Robert Harper wrote a book called *Psychoanalysis and Psychotherapy: 36 Schools* (Aronson, 1974). Several other schools have appeared since 1974. We cannot deal with all of them. Some that have caught the attention of the clergy are Gestalt Therapy, with its emphasis on the "here and now." Several of the non-Freudians have been read by the clergy, especially Karen Horney, Erich Fromm, and Harry Stack Sullivan.

The school that has attracted the largest following is Transactional Analysis (TA), due in part to the publication of a series of popular books such as *Games People Play, I'm OK—You're OK,* and *Born to Win.* A lot of pastors have become so attracted to TA that they have taken special training and become TA therapists. Transactional Analysis is basically a group approach and many of its concepts—such as the three ego states of parent, adult, and child, and the idea of playing games—can be applied to pastoral counseling.

Out of all this has emerged a great body of knowledge available to pastors for understanding their people. Pastors of local churches who are familiar with the different schools of thought will see manifestations of these theories in their parishioners every day. They will see people rationalizing, projecting, repressing their feelings. They will see parishioners with both healthy and unhealthy life-styles who feel inadequate. They will see introverts and extroverts in all areas of the church's life. They will see people acting irresponsibly and thinking irrationally. They will see people playing games with each other and operating out of the parent, adult, and child ego states. In other words, pastors are not psychologists and should not pretend to be, but the findings of the psychologists can help pastors understand the people in their congregation better and therefore meet their needs more effectively.

My own position in all this can be stated in three sentences:

1. All schools have some truth.
2. No school has all the truth.
3. None will replace the pastoral counselor.

I don't like the word *eclectic* because so many people are critical of it, as though it meant one is straddling the fence, unable to take a stand on either side, or has a watered-down accumulation of ideas with no real system or integrating factors. I disagree with the definition of an eclectic as "someone who has read two books." When I consulted *Webster's Dictionary,* I found *eclectic* defined as "what is thought best from various sources and systems." In that sense I am eclectic. Pastors owe it to the people with whom they are working to study and appropriate the best from whatever source.

As I have studied and observed the field of psychotherapy over many years, I have noticed that there are certain cycles that are almost predictable. When a new school of thought appears, it is usually the result of a strong personality who is either protesting or refining some previous school of thought. First, there is a period of experimentation when the new emphasis is relatively unnoticed and ignored. Next comes a period of disseminating these new ideas either in public address or in print. Then comes a period of gathering some followers who find this new approach promising, even exciting. This step is followed by a period of popularity, which results in a number of publications, perhaps a new organization with its own journal. During this time many people abandon old positions and jump on the bandwagon. Later on, the enthusiasm levels off; it is found that this system, too, has limitations; book sales decrease; people begin to look for new panaceas. Some of the new ideas are abandoned, but the ones that really prove effective are preserved and incorporated into the work of those who do not tie themselves to any one school but use the best of all for the good of their people.

## · F O U R ·

# Learning from the Psychotherapists: Methods and Techniques

One of the questions I am asked most frequently by pastors who consult me about pastoral problems in their churches is, "What should I *do* in this situation?" (or "What *should* I have done?"). They want practical answers; they are not interested in theories; they want to know what to do.

We used to call what a counselor did in a counseling situation a technique. I even taught a course entitled "Counseling Techniques." Now I am told that *technique* is no longer the accepted word. Now we should speak of counseling *strategies*. Techniques, strategies, methods, procedures, call it what you will, it all means the same thing. What does the parish pastor do when a person walks in the office and says, "I need help"?

Actually there are an amazing number of ways that people can be helped. This is due in large part to the phenomenal growth in the helping professions in recent years. All the various specialties have their own strategies: psychiatrists do, psychologists do, social workers do, marriage and family therapists do, school counselors do. Some of these are applicable to the pastoral counselor; some are not.

I became more aware of this phenomenon a few years ago when I was asked to lead a two-day pastors' conference. It was suggested that I should deal with pastoral counseling and psychotherapy and that it should be very practical in emphasis. I decided that on the first day I would discuss the methods of psychotherapists that could be used by the pastor, and on the second day I would discuss those methods or techniques (*strategies* still doesn't sound right for a pastor) that were unique to the pastoral counselor. I thought it might clarify things if I would duplicate a list of all of these methods, with a brief definition of each one, and put this list in the hands of the pastors attending the conference.

Much to my amazement the list totaled one hundred and ten. Even then, some of my colleagues were quick to point out that I had overlooked a few. Since this was done several years ago, there have been a few new techniques that have been tried and proven useful. I will include excerpts from that list at the close of this chapter.

There are not only many strategies for many problems, there are many strategies for helping people with the same problem. Take anxiety, for example. You can help persons reduce anxiety simply by listening attentively. As they pour out their anxious concerns, their anxiety often abates. Why this is we do not know, but there is ample evidence that it is so. You can help persons reduce anxiety by helping them to gain insight into the source or cause of the problem. When they understand its origin, they gain control over it. You can help persons overcome anxiety by training them to relax. Anxiety and relaxation are incompatible. You can help persons reduce anxiety by encouraging them to get regular exercise or take up a hobby they enjoy.

You can help persons reduce their anxiety by gradually exposing themselves to anxiety-inducing situations until they desensitize themselves to these situations. You can even help persons reduce anxiety by urging them to become more anxious—it is called paradoxical intention— and paradoxical as it sounds, it actually works. You can help persons overcome anxiety by training them in meditation, teaching them to pray, deepening their faith. The more persons are able to *trust*, the less anxious they will feel.

In actual practice, counseling methods all overlap and often are combined. For purposes of discussion I will divide them into nine separate groups or categories.

1. *Diagnostic techniques.* Actually I prefer the term *pastoral evaluation. Diagnosis* is a medical term, and I don't like to see the two roles confused. I discussed this with Paul Pruyser one time and he said, "Why don't you call it diagnosis? That's what you're doing." I bow to his wisdom. He also said that he is concerned that diagnosis seemed to be largely neglected in the literature of pastoral counseling. In fact, he made a survey to prove his point. He searched the tables of contents and the indices of all the books on pastoral counseling and pastoral care and found that the term was rarely even mentioned.

Some pastoral counselors have borrowed the history-taking procedures of the psychologist and the social worker. It is helpful to know people's backgrounds, ages, marital status, vocations, whether they were the oldest, youngest, or middle children, whether they have any physical problems, whether they are on medication, and whether they have consulted any other counselors. All such things give clues, as do tone of voice, facial expressions, manner of dress, and body language. The pastor of a local church usually has such information already and does not need an elaborate history-taking procedure.

Some pastoral counselors use the tools of the psychologists, such as psychological tests and personality inventories. The Minnesota Multiphasic Personality Inventory (MMPI) and the Taylor-Johnson Temperament Survey (TJ) are two of the most frequently used. Personally I have found the Incomplete Sentence Test provides me with more of the information I desire than most others. It should be pointed out that all such instruments are tools of the specialist and require special supervised training both to administer and to interpret them. They are subject to error and misinterpretation, and should be used only by those qualified and trained to do so—a safeguard that is all too often neglected.

Paul Pruyser contends that the pastor should diagnose peoples' concerns in terms of the pastor's own specialities, which are theology and religion. He even wrote a book about it: *The Minister as Diagnostician.* In this book he discusses seven guidelines, which he calls "diagnostic variables for pastoral assessment." These can be put in the form of questions pastors could have in mind as they work with their parishioners. They could ask themselves: Is this person aware of that which is holy? Does this person have a sense of the providence of God? Does this person have an experience of faith? Does this person have a sense of grace that results in feelings of gratitude? Is this person aware of the need of repentance? Does this person have a sense of communion or of kinship with all other people? Does this person have a sense of vocation? (Westminster Press, 1976, p. 61).

The idea of using theological concepts for evaluating a person's spiritual maturity is an intriguing one. It seems to me that such an idea is more practical as a guide for the pastor's own thinking than as a set of questions he or she could use with a parishioner. These are not familiar thought forms in our culture. Probably more counselors are familiar with the categories of the DSM-III (Diagnostic and Statistical Manual of Mental Disorders) than they are with biblical and theological concepts.

2. *Supportive techniques.* Historically, great pastors have usually been a source of support and reassurance to their parishioners. A pastor, by virtue of his or her role in the community, may be the one most qualified to render support.

William A. Clebsch and Charles R. Jaekle in their book *Pastoral Care in Historical Perspective* contend that there are four basic functions that pastors have provided in every epoch of the church's history. These are healing, sustaining, guiding, and reconciling.

It is sustaining that has been one of the church's greatest contributions. Contemporary literature uses the word *supportive.* It means the same thing. Some object to the word *support* because it may imply weakness. I do not use it in that sense. I mean by *support* the same thing Clebsch and Jaekle are talking about when they say that pastors have always been sustaining people. Rather than resulting in weakness, it provides strength.

There are many methods that provide support. Statements of reassurance, encouragement, just a word, a look, may communicate understanding, confidence, and strength. Providing information when needed, offering a brief prayer, or reading a verse of Scripture all provide support. Just being present during a difficult situation may be of great help. Support has been referred to as the ministry of standing by. It should never be minimized. The pastor should be a specialist in providing support and reassurance.

3. *Insight-achieving techniques.* In the early days of the counseling movement, insight was the primary goal of all counseling. It was felt that if a person had insight, the problem was largely solved. It was later found that that was not always true, but even so, insight usually helps. In pastoral counseling, insight is still one of the major objectives.

Insight is the capacity to understand ourselves, both intellectually and emotionally, to understand others, or to understand a situation. Usually the more insight we have, the more understanding we have of others. In counseling and psychotherapy, insight helps persons become aware of underlying motives and unconscious sources of their feelings, problems, and behavior.

Insight may seem to come suddenly. People sometimes have flashes of insight. This is the well-known "aha" effect that results from a seemingly sudden grasp of relationships, that explains a situation or leads to the resolution of a problem or to the achievement of better self-understanding. More often it is a gradual process in which we acquire understanding in small steps. Even when our insight appears to be sudden, it usually was preceded by much searching and tension.

4. *Behavior-change techniques.* Behavior-change techniques are just that, methods that have been designed to change behavior and that is all. Through the centuries pastors have attempted to change behavior primarily by preaching and giving good advice. With the advent of the learning theorists mentioned in the previous chapter, a whole group of methods and techniques were made available by which behavior could be altered or changed: assertiveness training, systematic desensitization, graduated exposure, satiation, role playing, imaginative practice, thought stopping, and many, many more. All of these are for the purpose of changing behavior; the learning theorists were not interested in insight, support, or dealing with symptoms. The symptom was seen as the problem. These were all methods to change maladaptive behavior to more appropriate acceptable behavior. Some of these methods are applicable in pastoral counseling; some are not.

As important as knowing some of the specific techniques with which to change behavior is being familiar with the principles with which they are applied. We should remember to assign only those behavioral tasks in which people are likely to be successful. Behavior is usually changed by small steps. There is such a thing as one trial learning, but it is usually done over a period of time. We begin with simple tasks where success is likely and gradually progress to more difficult learning. All healthy behavior is rewarded and reinforced. Negative or neurotic behavior is ignored or corrected. Whereas the behavior modification counselors use these methods exclusively, the pastor does not need to be so limited. The pastor can use behavioral assignments to be done between sessions, while the counseling hour is devoted to such things as support and insight.

5. *Cognitive techniques.* The cognitive therapists have developed procedures through which the parishioners (patients/clients) monitor their own thoughts, evaluate them, and develop more healthy responses. This is usually done on paper, between sessions. In essence the counselees become their own therapists. The counselor is a teacher, trainer, and guide. The counselees are taught both the principles and the methods they will follow. It is an oversimplification to be sure, but basically this consists of three steps: (1) identifying the thoughts that are causing the discomfort, (2) evaluating these thoughts in terms of what is irrational or unrealistic about them, (3) replacing them with more healthy, acceptable ideas. Ellis and Maltsby call this the A-B-C theory of the emotions. The event is A; it can be any event, large or small. The thoughts we have about A is B. The feeling we have as a result of B is C. It is not A that makes us angry or nervous; it is what we think about A that produces the negative or positive results. This is a method that has proven very practical in pastoral counseling. A bit of ancient wisdom says, "For as he thinketh in his heart, so is he" (Prov. 23:7 KJV).

6. *Educative techniques.* Counseling is basically a learning experience, although sometimes the learning is more emotional than it is intellectual. Jesus was a teacher. The pastor also is a teacher. The class may be one person or one couple, and the classroom is the pastor's study. There are some persons who need information. They have insufficient knowledge to make mature decisions or to understand a situation. The information they have may be out-of-date, incomplete, or inaccurate. Pastors may provide this information verbally, or they may provide reading materials that broaden a person's perspective, or may refer

them to someone or some group who can give them the needed information. Whatever the method in educative counseling, the laws of learning apply just as much as they do in a graduate seminar or a lecture hall.

7. *Growth-counseling methods.* The emphasis of counseling and psychotherapy up until recent days has been on helping the neurotic, the maladjusted, move up to the normal or average level (if there is any such thing as normal or average). It is now being recognized that it is equally important to take persons who are functioning well at the normal or average level and help them move up to a more creative level where they can render a larger service, find deeper meanings in life, and experience greater joy and satisfaction. This, too, must be done on an individual, one-to-one basis, where the pastor takes persons with their own unique talents, interests, and opportunities and helps them find those methods and those insights that enable them to find life ever more creative and meaningful. A long time ago William James taught us that most people do not live within sight of their possibilities. Among the pastoral counselors, Howard Clinebell has been giving growth counseling a great deal of attention lately. Hopefully, others will follow. This may be the next step forward for the counseling movement.

8. *Religious techniques or spiritual disciplines.* The pastor is first of all a minister and should be a specialist in utilizing both Christian beliefs and Christian practices. Chapter 10 is devoted to this discussion.

9. *Supplementary techniques.* There are many things that a person can be asked to do between sessions that supplement what is done in the counseling hour. These supplementary techniques take many forms—assigned

reading, relaxation exercises, tasks to perform—or some of the spiritual disciplines mentioned elsewhere. Certain principles should be followed when making such assignments as they are supplementary to the counseling and do not replace it. The assignments must be selected to fit the needs and interests of the counselee. Not all persons want to read or meditate; not everyone wants to jog or do free writing. It is better if the pastor and the parishioner share in the selection of the things to be done between sessions. Assignments should be made that are realistic and likely to be achieved successfully. Little is accomplished if such assignments are sporadic and occasional. Assignments are most successful when an individual plan is developed and pursued regularly. The best results occur when time is preserved to discuss what has taken place and the results are incorporated in the counseling sessions.

Now we will include a few of the definitions that were in the list of one hundred ten. The only technique in this list that is original with me is the one described as the "floundering" technique. It came about this way. I had been working with a family for a long time. Nothing seemed to help. I consulted with a psychiatrist about it, hoping he could give me some guidance. I said, "I've tried everything I know. Nothing seems to work." He asked, "Do you like these people?" I said, "Very much, that is why I would like to help." He said, "Are they still coming?" I said, "Yes, they never miss an appointment." He said, "Keep on floundering around. Some day they will get better. You won't know why, but that really doesn't matter." So it proved to be.

Many times when pastors have come to me to discuss situations they were dealing with and were feeling the same frustrations I was feeling, I have said, "Just keep floundering around; someday they will get better. You won't know why, but that doesn't really matter."

I obviously am not going to include all one hundred ten definitions, but will list some of them alphabetically as examples of the many ways there are to help.

*Advice.* A procedure in which the counselor makes a definite recommendation regarding a decision or a course of action.

*Archetypes.* The explanation of behavior in terms of universal thought forms.

*Art and Drawing.* The use of drawing or artistic productions both as a diagnostic tool and as a means of reducing tension and expressing creativity.

*Assertive Responses.* A method in which the counselor urges the counselee to act assertively, in a socially acceptable way, in a situation that has been producing anxiety.

*Assets and Liabilities List.* A procedure whereby the counselee is asked to list his or her ten major assets and liabilities, which gives the counselor a quick evaluation of the counselee's self-concept and also provides a basis for discussion.

*Assignments.* The procedure of giving the counselee some tasks to perform between sessions.

*Behavior Rehearsal.* A procedure in which the counselee is asked to act out a role or responsibility that causes tension, in anticipation of doing it in actual experience.

*Bibliotherapy.* The assignment of reading materials to provide information and foster personal growth.

*Case History.* The case history has long been recognized as a diagnostic tool. It also has therapeutic value in that those counselees filling in the items about themselves often gain insight into their significance.

*Catharsis.* The process whereby a person is encouraged to bring an unconscious drive or experience to consciousness, thus releasing tension and freeing the person from repressed drives or experiences.

*Confession.* The verbalization of sins or weaknesses to a pastor, usually in search of forgiveness.

*Conjoint Counseling.* The process of seeing all the members of a family simultaneously.

*Confrontation.* A counseling technique by which the counselor confronts the counselee with an issue or a situation in order to make him or her aware of the implications, explanations, or possibilities that are present.

*Covenant (Contract) of Counseling.* A procedure whereby the counselee is asked to make a commitment to the counseling process and procedure.

*De-reflection.* A process whereby a person is asked to ignore certain problems and focus attention away from himself or herself, especially on matters that have meaning.

*Dream Interpretation.* The use of dreams to help a person understand inner dynamics.

*Environmental Manipulation.* A process whereby the counselor helps the counselee make alterations in the situation that is causing or contributing to the difficulty.

*Exercise.* The assignment of physical activity to reduce tension and promote a feeling of physical and emotional well-being.

*Floundering Technique.* The process of using all the knowledge and skill we possess, though the counselor is not sure what method to apply or what procedure to follow—but keeps on trying.

*Free Writing.* A method in which counselees are asked to express themselves on paper to reduce tension, clarify thinking, and lead to insight.

*Graduated Exposure.* A procedure in which counselees are directed to attempt a series of tasks that have previously produced tension, or that can lead to the development of new strengths. The tasks should be simple at first and increase in difficulty.

*Group Counseling.* A method of using groups to help people gain a sense of belonging, improve communication, secure the support and guidance of the group, and deepen understanding and insight. (This can include group guidance, group therapy, and growth groups.)

*Humor.* The use of humor to relieve tension and to help gain perspective. Diagnostically, a person's sense of humor provides clues to personality needs.

*Interpretation.* The process whereby a counselor attempts to assist in gaining understanding and insight by interpreting some of the causes of relationships he or she feels are important.

*Life Goal Selection.* A procedure in which the counselor assists the counselee in selecting reasonable, realistic life goals.

*Life-style Analysis.* A process in which the counselor analyzes the life-style of the counselees to understand their needs, to predict possible development, and to help in creating a life-style that is more healthy and creative.

*Listening.* A procedure in which the counselor listens attentively to establish rapport, release tension, and lead to insight.

*Logotherapy* (The Quest for Meaning). The process in which counselees are helped to find meaning in their lives or in specific situations.

*Music Therapy.* The use of music as a supportive method or as an adjunct to other forms of therapy.

*Negative Practice.* A method whereby counselees are required to practice the behavior they want to eliminate extensively until such practice leads to its extinction.

*Occupational Therapy.* The providing of tasks and creative work opportunities to reduce tension, build confidence, and help counselees attain insight.

*Paradoxical Intention.* A method in which counselees are asked to "intend" or create that which they fear.

*Persuasion.* A procedure whereby the counselor definitely attempts to persuade a person to follow a certain course of action.

*Poetry Therapy.* The reading and writing of poetry, both for diagnostic and therapeutic purposes. Can be done individually or in groups.

*Prescribed Sentences.* A procedure of prescribing brief, concise sentences selected to meet each person's needs, which would interrupt or counteract the conditioning that has resulted in neurotic thoughts or behavior.

*Questioning.* The use of questions to secure more information, or to help counselees weigh alternatives or evaluate their own situations.

*Reassurance.* The process, usually verbal, of providing assurance and affirming a person, thereby increasing confidence and building strength.

*Recreation Therapy.* The use of recreational activities as tension-reducing techniques or as adjuncts to other forms of therapy.

*Reflection of Feelings.* The process of entering into the inner frame of reference of a counselee in order to understand his or her feelings and then reflecting these feelings back to the person in order to develop a sense of being understood and accepted.

*Relaxation Therapy.* The use of muscular relaxation to aid in the reducing of tension.

*Role Playing.* A procedure in which counselees act out a role, either their own or that of someone else, to help them understand themselves and others.

*Self-disclosure.* The process whereby the counselor shares with the counselee the fact that he or she has had similar or related problems.

*Supportive Therapy.* A method of supporting a person by providing reassurance, encouragement, and guidance to reduce tensions and build on strengths.

*Systematic Desensitization.* A method of reducing tension by presenting scenes in the imagination that have previously caused tension but when presented in a state of physical and emotional relaxation, the tension is reduced.

*Thought Control.* A method of reducing anxiety and developing confidence through the disciplined control of thoughts.

*Thought Interruption.* A procedure for interrupting continuous negative or unrealistic thoughts.

*Time Projection.* A procedure whereby counselees are asked to visualize themselves at some time in the future in order to gain understanding of goals and desires.

*Transference.* The use of the transference phenomenon in helping persons gain self-understanding.

Responsible pastors will keep abreast of new developments in counseling and psychotherapy in order to deepen their understanding of human behavior and to sharpen their counseling skills so they will be able to render greater service.

# · F I V E ·

# Pastoral Counseling
# with University Students

John R. Mott once said that if he had his life to live over again, he would place himself alongside a university campus, for there were the greatest needs and the greatest opportunities in the world. Anyone who has worked with students knows what he meant. They have great individual and personal needs. They have unlimited possibilities. Counseling university students is a great challenge and an awesome responsibility.

Does Mott's statement mean that only those pastors whose parishes adjoin a college campus do student counseling? Not at all. It is true that some pastors have more of an opportunity to work with students than others, but almost all pastors do on occasion. After all, there are over nine million students in America's colleges and universities.

Because of my interest in students, I chose as the topic for my doctoral dissertation, "The Religious Counseling of University Students." (This was later revised, rewritten, and published under the title *Counseling with College Students,* Prentice Hall, 1964. Much of the material is dated. I hope that someone will do a more thorough and contemporary volume.)

When I began my research I discovered a strange phenomenon. When I went to the library to locate source materials, I went first to the pastoral counseling section, with which I was most familiar. There were many good books on pastoral counseling but none on the pastoral counseling of students. The fact was, when I explored both the tables of contents and indices, students or the campus were almost never mentioned. It was as though they didn't exist as an area of concern by pastoral counselors.

Next I turned to the books on counseling university students. There was an abundance of them. Darley, Williamson, Robinson, and others had done their work well—except at one point. They almost completely overlooked the significance of religion in the life of a student, and the church or the pastor as a source of referral. There were a few exceptions, but in the main, this is a gap that has not been resolved to this day.

Very few seminaries have courses in counseling with university students and to my knowledge there are few, if any, CPE programs on university campuses.

We will discuss this very important area by looking first at the pastor, then the student, and finally the campus.

Every pastor, no matter how remote his or her parish, is a potential student counselor. All churches, rural or urban, downtown or suburban, large or small, have in their membership young people who complete secondary school and attend college. This is more true today than it has ever been in any previous generation.

The pastor has an exceptional opportunity to prepare students for college, to counsel them as they face the questions of the value of a college education, the choice of a school and a major field of study, and everything that pertains to moving from high school to higher education. Some have conflicts with their parents about the value of going to school, or where to go. Many capable students doubt their ability to do advanced work. Some need financial help; others are quite unprepared academically, emotionally, or spiritually for the experience.

The pastor has an advantage that no university counselor or university pastor has, of knowing their background, knowing their families, and having a previous relationship with them. If the church is not in the same community as the campus, there is the disadvantage of being separated from the students for a period of time. Even here, communication need not be completely shut off. A concerned pastor can keep in touch with students by correspondence. A student can write to a pastor in moments of discouragement or indecision, and when the student returns home during vacations, he or she may seek the pastor for counseling or guidance.

The pastor of a university church has the same responsibilities as any other pastor toward the young people in the church who plan to attend college, plus the added responsibility of ministering to students in the university community where the church is located. These students may come from all parts of the country, even all parts of the world. Many will attend the services of worship. If the pastor preaches with understanding, as though he or she was aware of the students' needs, if the pastor has the reputation of one who understands students, many will seek his or her counsel. That pastor's church will become the "church home away from home" for many students.

The pastor in a university church has the very real advantage of being available. The students need not depend on correspondence or a trip home to see the pastor. That pastor also has the advantage of knowing the college atmosphere, being acquainted with university personnel, as well as having a familiarity with sources of referral on the campus. While the university pastor does not have the advantage of knowing the student's family, he or she does have the advantage of anonymity. Many students will discuss problems with a pastor in another community who would not feel free to discuss these same problems with their own pastor who also happens to be their parents' pastor.

More recently there has developed a group of specialists whose only responsibility is to minister to students. These consist of university pastors who represent denominations and are assigned to serve students, staff members of university churches whose primary responsibilities are to serve as ministers to students, and university chaplains, or ministers to the university. All these have the advantage that they devote their full time to a ministry to students. They do not have to divide their time with sermon preparation, church administration, or ministering to a congregation other than students.

The minister to students, whether on the staff of a university church or representing a denomination, has the advantage of being a part of the university but is not associated with such matters as student discipline or assigning grades. The fact that such positions are usually supported by a denomination has both advantages and disadvantages. The chaplain or minister to the university has an ecumenical ministry but may have some barriers in that he or she is identified with the administration. At the same time, this has some advantages in that this person does have a natural relationship with the university personnel services and, on some campuses, is considered a part of the personnel staff and, in a few, a member of the counseling staff.

The pastor, in whatever of the above positions, who is working on or near a campus is working in a distinctive atmosphere and with a select group of people. A college or university has a society all its own; it has its status systems, in-groups and out-groups, cultural and vocational interests, its own folkways, customs, traditions, and taboos. The one thing that ties all these things together is that the university is an academic institution, organized and maintained for educational purposes.

All counseling must be seen in terms of the framework of the institution in which the counselor works. This is true whether it is a hospital, the army, a retirement center, or a university. So, first of all, the pastor must know the world of the campus. This is the world in which the student lives. This is where many of the student's problems arise and where they must be worked out.

To know the modern campus is not easy—campuses differ. There is quite a difference between the atmosphere of a state university with thousands of students in the entering class and the atmosphere of a small denominational college with only a few hundred enrolled overall. There is a marked contrast between an Ivy League school in the East and a small community college in the Southwest, between a municipal university and an agricultural college. There are also differences between different colleges on the same university campus, and even between different departments in the same college. The difference can be very great between philosophy majors and business majors, between students in the physical education department planning on a career of coaching and students in fine arts, or those preparing for theological school.

According to the sociologists, students comprise a definite and distinctive subgroup in our society, but it is deceiving to think of them as all having common characteristics and patterns. Some are freshmen, new and confused; some are seniors or graduate students, sophisticated as to the ways of the campus. Some are on academic probation; some are on the dean's list, candidates for Phi Beta Kappa. Some are homesick; others are glad to be free from the restraints of parents. Some are wrapped up in fraternity and social life; some are totally uninterested and look upon Greek-letter societies with disdain. Some are primarily interested in athletics, some in drama, some in ethical and philosophical issues. Some have clear-cut vocational goals and ambitions; others have no vocational goals at all. Some find it necessary to work to scrape together enough to pay tuition and books; others are the children of wealthy parents and drive their own convertibles to the campus. Some are married; some have children to care for; others are single. Some are well-adjusted and mature; others are quite immature, subject to constant anxiety and stress. Some are very popular, living in a social whirl; others prefer to be alone. Still others spend weekends in the dorm—not by choice, but because no one asks them out. Some find college challenging and exciting; others find it boring and tedious. Who is the student? The student is all these things and more.

Pastoral counseling with students is largely counseling with an age group. This isn't entirely true, for some older persons return to college (and in graduate school, the majority are older), but in the main, college students represent later adolescence and young adulthood. In counseling students, we also deal with a select group intellectually, those who have continued education beyond high school. A gradual screening process has taken place, beginning with those who graduate from high school, continuing on through college entrance requirements and the freshman year of college. Those who survive are, to a considerable degree, at the top level of the intellectual curve. This is even more true when you consider graduate students.

First-year students are living in a new environment; very often they are away from home for the first time. Moral restraints of home, church, and community are gone, and homesickness may be very real. If the student comes from a small town and a small high school, the freshman class may be larger than his or her entire high school. The student is confronted with a wide variety of social, athletic, and cultural activities outside the classroom. The demands on a student's time may be terrific, and many of them face this problem without previous experience in organizing and planning their time and without enough personal self-discipline to stay with a plan for an entire semester. The demands are even greater if the student has to work to pay expenses. It is no wonder that students are often bewildered and confused.

It is commonly recognized that religious problems are often accentuated on a college campus. Some students are faced with the necessity of completely reorienting their thinking. In many cases it may be the students' first contact with points of view other than their own. It may be the first time students have heard the beliefs of their home church, or the church of their parents, challenged or debated. This problem is further complicated by the fact that so many students come to the campus with a limited background or training in things religious. Their Sunday school training is insufficient for the intellectual challenge of the campus. This generalization may be unfair to some students and to some churches, but anyone who has worked with students is aware of how common this problem is.

Such problems can cause students real stress, often accompanied by anxiety and guilt. They are struggling with new ideas, which may create tensions with their parents. The pastor is the one most qualified to deal with such matters. In fact, these religious and theological concerns are areas that some university counseling services try to avoid.

Because of the age group mentioned above, it is a time in life when all the problems of courtship and marriage are present. Premarital counseling has been discussed so thoroughly in so many places that we need not elaborate on it here. Suffice it to say that anyone who would work with students should recognize that this will be a major responsibility. Since more and more students are married while in college, and the majority in graduate school are married, this means that the pastor who works with students must be prepared to do considerable marriage counseling as well. This includes all the traditional problems of marriage counseling, plus the ones that are unique to the campus, not the least of which is the problem of earning a living, raising a family, paying tuition, and finding some time for each other.

While the pastor is concerned primarily about religious, personal, and family matters, the students also are concerned with educational problems. Educational programs are directly related to future vocational goals and achievements. Many professional counselors feel that the pastor should move with extreme caution in educational or vocational counseling. We will deal with the latter in another section. Some prefer that the pastor not enter these two fields at all. They have reason for their words of caution. Educational counseling is a highly complicated field that requires some specialized skills. Correctly applied, it requires a knowledge of psychological tests and their interpretation and a thorough knowledge of the curriculum, both as to specific courses and general fields of study. Educational counseling requires a knowledge of such techniques as study habits, reading skills and comprehension, and research procedures. It demands an acquaintance with scholarship sources, speech clinics, school practices, rules, and traditions.

Pastors must recognize their limitations and work within their own area of competence, and call on the help of specialists when it is needed. At the same time, pastors cannot completely separate themselves from some responsibility in the educational experience of the students who seek help. Some students who cannot be persuaded to go to the university counseling center will go to their pastor. Some of the problems that are of a religious or personal nature may have academic implications. It is not uncommon for a student to go to his or her pastor with a problem of dissatisfaction with an educational plan or a vocational goal.

Other students may have feelings of inadequacy and discouragement that have an important relationship to their educational progress. Many things hinder optimal educational achievement other than ability or study habits—anxiety or guilt over moral questions; worry over financial, social, or family conflicts; adolescent revolt against authority; or emotional conflict over religious or philosophical questions. These are more likely to be taken to a pastor than to a faculty member or university counselor. Here the pastor can be of service both to the students and to the university's personnel services.

To go back to John R. Mott's statement that a university campus is one of the most important places in society: Here are gathered together some of the brightest and most capable young adults in America. It is a period in their lives when they face many tensions and are making choices and decisions that will affect their entire futures. When we deal with students, we know that what we do here may have far-reaching effects, both in those lives and in the lives of many others. It is the students on our campuses today who will be the leaders of the world tomorrow.

The statesmen, the scientists, the community leaders, the religious leaders of tomorrow are in the colleges and universities of today.

Whenever a pastor has the privilege of working with one of these capable students, the pastor not only has the awareness that he or she is helping a person to resolve some immediate tension or conflict, but that he or she is also helping to guide a young person who may have great potential for good in the future, perhaps someone who can make greater contributions than the pastor can make. This is a humbling and exciting thought. It is both a challenge and an opportunity.

# Pastoral Counseling and the Vocational Guidance Movement

A man just left my office. He is forty-one, very discouraged. He is changing jobs, but he doesn't think he will like his new one. It offers no challenge but he says, "You have to do something." After he left, I reflected on many others who have told me similar stories. A young woman wondered if she should quit her job. It paid well; it required nothing illegal but it did require some things she felt were unethical. It troubled her conscience, but jobs were scarce and she needed the money. A sophomore in the university was in the engineering program, but he didn't want to be an engineer. He said, "My father is an engineer; my uncle is an engineer; everyone in my family has to be an engineer, but I want to teach." A high school senior, active in the youth program of the church, said, "I would really like to study for the ministry, but I feel so unworthy." A man in his mid-forties said, "What I'd really like to do is sell my business and go to seminary, but I've got two kids ready for college and I'm not sure my wife would be willing to give up the house and the standard of living we now have." A schoolteacher said, "I love to teach, but it doesn't pay enough to meet our needs. I hate to give it up. I'm a good teacher, but I have no choice." A college freshman says, "I'm supposed to declare my major, but I haven't the slightest idea what I want to do when I graduate."

These are not verbatim statements, but they are all based on real situations. They all have two things in common. These persons all had concerns about vocational choice or adjustment, and they all discussed them with a pastor.

The surveys I have read indicate that these are very common problems. Studies indicate that young people are more concerned about their vocational future than they are with almost any other subject. Studies of adults indicate that more than half the adults are unhappy in their work and a large percentage would choose something else to do if they had their lives to live over again. This seems very sad.

There can be no question about the importance of vocational choice and adjustment. It is one of the most important decisions a person ever makes. It is a decision that affects a person's whole future.

The first factor usually mentioned is an economic one. The ability to earn a living is a mark of maturity in our culture. Our economic security and, to a certain extent, our standard of living is contingent upon a wise vocational choice.

More than a person's economic well-being is involved, however. A person's identity is largely determined by the work he or she does. When we make a new acquaintance, one of the first questions we usually ask is what does he or she do? We have a different opinion of that person if he or she is a doctor, a preacher, a U.S. senator, a used car salesman, or a professional football player.

A person's vocation also has much to do with his or her psychological and emotional well-being. Michaelangelo said, "It is only well with me when there is a chisel in my hand." There is a procedure used in veterans' and mental hospitals called occupational therapy. It has been found that just making a leather belt is better than doing nothing. There is a healing power in work.

Persons who have found work they really enjoy are most fortunate. Work that challenges our abilities, work that we feel is meaningful and worthwhile adds great satisfaction to life as a whole. President Charles Eliot of Harvard used to say, "Harvard pays me for doing things I would gladly do for nothing if it were necessary." Such an attitude toward one's job is a great possession.

Much is said about the value of self-esteem. What is not so frequently realized is that our self-esteem is largely dependent on the work we do. If we feel our work is unimportant, that it is something to be embarrassed about, or apologetic about, then it can be a source of real emotional conflict. People who find their work boring, dull, unchallenging, that this is all they have to look forward to day after day, year after year, are susceptible to real emotional problems. If our work does not demand our natural abilities, or if it requires more ability than we have—in either case, stress and tension result.

To carry this one step further, many say that life has to have meaning. We all need to feel that our lives count. Our sense of meaning is closely associated with the work we do. This isn't all that gives life meaning, however. Some are caught in dead-end jobs where little meaning can be found in what they do. They need to be helped to find meaning in other areas of life. If a person can find work that does have value, does render a service, does give life meaning, that person is most fortunate and should be grateful.

It is frequently said, "It is more important to make a life than to make a living." In a certain sense, this is true. What this phrase overlooks is the fact that the way we make a living often determines a way of life. When persons choose a vocation, they also choose a way of life. They will have quite a different life if they choose to be a farmer, a foreign diplomat, an FBI agent, a football coach, or a minister of the gospel. Their vocational choice determines where they will live, what clothes they will wear, what professional organizations they will belong to, and how they will be perceived by other people.

The choice of a vocation is not only an individual matter, but is important to society as well. Every year more than two million young people leave school and enter the job market. There are so many moral and spiritual needs in the world that it is important that some of these young people find places in society through which some of these needs can be met.

It is obvious from what has been said thus far that I feel vocational concern is a legitimate part of pastoral counseling. Not all vocational counselors would agree. I once conducted a survey of vocational counselors across the country to find out for myself their attitudes toward pastoral counselors. The responses were pretty clear. The majority do not feel pastors should be doing vocational counseling.

Considering the nature of vocational counseling, we can understand why they feel as they do. Vocational counseling as a specialty is of fairly recent origin, but its practitioners have developed some highly specialized skills. There have been a number of significant changes since Frank Parsons first combined the two words *vocational* and *guidance* about 1906.

In the early days of the movement, vocational counseling consisted primarily of giving counselees good advice about what vocation to follow. But it was advice based on sound and thorough clinical procedures. The two basic processes were: (1) understanding the individual, and (2) understanding the world of work.

Information about the individual was gained by the usual methods of observation, the interview, school records, work experience, plus references and thorough testing procedures. Vocational guidance leaned heavily on the mental measurement movement.

Counselors used mental ability tests, vocational interest tests, vocational aptitude tests, and personality inventories. Only on the basis of these standardized measures did they presume to make a decision.

They also developed extensive procedures for understanding the world of work. This was known as occupational information. This information had to measure up to definite standards. It had to be thorough, complete, accurate, and up-to-date.

On the basis of their evaluation of the individual and "occupational info," the candidate was given sound clinical advice. The early definitions of vocational counseling defined it as advising people what they ought to do.

Then due to the influence of developments in psychotherapy, giving advice fell into disfavor. Definitions of the vocational guidance process changed to (1) helping the individual understand himself or herself, and (2) helping the individual understand the world of work, so that he or she could make a mature decision, based on sound self-understanding and accurate information. Only then would the decision be both wise and, hopefully, permanent.

The reason my respondents were hesitant about pastors venturing into this field was that pastors are not trained to give or interpret vocational tests, and they do not have access to up-to-date information about job requirements or job opportunities.

The fact remains that many people, like the ones quoted at the beginning of this chapter, do go to a pastor to discuss their career concerns. In some cases there is no one else to go to. There are hundreds of young adults who are not in school and have nowhere else to turn. Increasing numbers of people in the so-called middle years are facing a mid-life career change, often a decision that causes considerable stress.

These people don't have access to a counseling center, as university students do. They don't need a psychiatrist; they don't need a doctor, but they do need someone to talk to. Also, many discussions that start out as a discussion of marriage or religious problems soon are seen to involve vocational implications. The opposite is also true. Many discussions that start out as a discussion of vocational concerns are soon found to have marriage, ethical, and religious implications.

Even of those in high school or college where guidance counselors are available, only a small percentage receive any extensive vocational guidance at all. That's not a criticism, but only a statement of fact. In the average city high school of three thousand students or more, there is no way the staff of counselors can provide adequate vocational guidance to more than a small percentage of the students. The same thing is true on the campus of any major university.

Some of these persons, because they have a good relationship with a pastor, will discuss their vocational and career concerns with the pastor. When this occurs, the pastor needs to heed the warning of the vocational counselor; he or she should never guess at a person's abilities and aptitudes. How does the pastor know that this person will be admitted to medical school? The same thing is true of occupational information. What are the projected needs in the future? Where is the training received? What are the satisfactions and dissatisfactions? What are the projected salary ranges, the retirement benefits, and so forth? The pastor can't be expected to know this information about all the jobs and professions. What the pastor does need to know is where the measurements can be secured and where the information is available.

There are other reasons why the pastor has a concern about vocations and careers. After all, *vocation* is a theological word. That is the way Luther used it. It is a "calling." If God is concerned about all of life, he is concerned about what a person does from Monday to Friday as well as what he or she does from 11:00 to 12:00 on Sunday morning. Our vocation may include much more than the way we make a living. That is biblical, too. Amos was a shepherd and a dresser of sycamore trees. That was his occupation; it wasn't his vocation. Paul was a tentmaker by trade and apparently pursued it throughout his ministry, but it wasn't his vocation. Vocational counselors meet a real need, but few of them stress the theological dimensions of vocation or emphasize the need for service.

The pastor must emphasize the place of work in our total life philosophy. The pastor should help develop attitudes that dignify all work. The pastor must help people see a life as a vocation.

There is another area where the pastor is a specialist, and this is the whole field of church vocations, where young people (and some not so young) are considering the ministry, religious education, the chaplaincy, missions, or other branches of church service.

Vocational counselors, as a rule, do not want to get involved in this specialized field. In the survey I mentioned earlier, 90 percent felt pastors should not be doing vocational guidance. When I asked about counseling candidates for the ministry, 90 percent said they would prefer that pastors do it. The vocational counselors are not familiar with the wide variety of faiths—Catholic, Protestant, and Jewish. They are not acquainted with requirements for ordination or prospects for employment when it is attained. They are unfamiliar with the concept of the "call." When a student is considering medicine or law, he or she decides to become a doctor or an attorney. Pastors feel they are "called" to the ministry. There are many beliefs about what this call means. When I did a little book for the National Council of Churches on "preparing for the ministry," it had to clear all the participating denominations. The chapter that had the most difficulty was the one on "the call." Vocational counselors aren't even sure what a minister does. The pastor is known as a preacher. The preaching aspect is seen in public, but the caring, counseling, administrative tasks are largely unknown. Here the pastor is the specialist on this specialized area of occupational information. Both the welfare of the individual and the welfare of the church in general are involved. At times the pastor has to counsel people away from the ministry as well as help them decide for it.

Vocational counseling must be seen as a process—not just an interview. A mature vocational choice must be made over a period of time, not in a few counseling sessions. The person starts with a lot of uncertainty, considers many alternatives, weighs and evaluates each, considers his or her own strengths and limitations, gains information, starts training, usually experiences some frustration and self-doubt, continues until the decision is firm, the training is secured, and the position is attained. The pastor stands by the person in the process, explores the possibilities, makes suggestions, listens a lot, encourages on occasion, and is always aware that vocational counseling is a sacred and far-reaching responsibility.

# Pastoral Counseling with Exceptional Persons

In the twenty-fifth chapter of Matthew, Jesus told a story commonly referred to as the parable of the talents. It says, "For it will be as when a man going on a journey called his servants and entrusted to them his property; to one he gave five talents, to another two, to another one, to each according to his ability" (Matt. 25:14-15). The findings of intelligence tests are not new. What is new is a method of measuring ability by the use of standardized methods, usually referred to as mental ability tests or intelligence tests. These tests give a person an IQ score, or a percentile rank score, depending on the type of test, which indicates a person's brightness, mental ability, or scholastic aptitude— all of which mean essentially the same thing.

Extensive study and research also reveal that these different levels of mental ability are distributed through the general population according to the normal bell-shaped curve. That is, about 1 percent would be at the top of the scale with an IQ of 130 or above and about 1 percent would be at the bottom of the scale with an IQ of 70 or below. The rest would be distributed equally with about the same number on each side of the median, which is 100.

If a pastor could give a mental abilities test to all the members of the congregation, it would reveal that there is a small group that could be classified as gifted and a larger group that could be known educationally as rapid learners. We are talking about 1 to 5 percent of the congregation. These figures would vary somewhat with the location of the church. There would be a larger percentage of gifted in a college congregation, for example. The largest number would be in the middle or average range, from 90 to 110. This would include about 60 percent of the group if they divide according to national averages. At the other end of the scale from the gifted would be a group of similar size that would be considered retarded or slow learners.

By way of illustration, let's take two young people in the congregation and call them A and B. A has an IQ of 133. That puts him in the top 1 percent of the population. B has an IQ of 69 or 70. That puts him or her in the bottom 1 percent of the population. In New Testament terms, A has five talents, B has one. In educational or psychological terms, A is gifted, B is retarded, or at least borderline.

If both are twelve years of age, then A has a mental age of sixteen, but B has a mental age of eight. When both are fifteen, A will have a mental age of twenty, but B will have a mental age of ten. By the time they are adults, A will probably have finished college and entered business or one of the professions, while B will probably have dropped out of school and be doing some form of manual labor.

These are not exceptions. Of couse, 1 percent seems like a small number, until we think of it in terms of the nation, the community, or even one conregation. It is estimated that there are between thirty and forty million school children in America. That means that over three hundred thousand are in the top 1 percent. At the other end of the scale the same thing holds true: There are more than three hundred thousand retarded children of school age. If we include the next 5 percent, those at the top of the scale who are listed as rapid learners or very bright, and those at the bottom of the scale whose intelligence is a bit below average or slow learners, we have now added to the figures by thousands, even millions. To bring it down to our concern for the ministry and the church, if a pastor has a congregation of five hundred, by national averages that pastor will have from five to twenty-five persons who are very brilliant, and an equal number whose mental ability is well below the general average. Both groups have special needs. Both groups are very important; both groups need a ministry.

Let's take the group at the top part of the curve first. As I have written before, the pastor is concerned about the persons for three reasons: (1) Because of the good they can do—if these people can be challenged to use their great talents in Christian service or for the common good, the pastor may be instrumental in helping someone make a contribution far greater than anything the pastor could have done. This is a thrilling thought. (2) The pastor is also concerned because of the harm they can do. A smart crook can do more damage than a stupid one. History is full of the tragic records of brilliant persons who had no sense of moral values or concern for the common good. (3) The pastor is concerned about these persons primarily because as persons, they have needs just like everyone else, and some that are created by their very giftedness.

One of the primary difficulties of the gifted is socialization. They often find it difficult to find congenial companionship. Take any teenage youngster with an IQ of 130 or above and almost invariably you will find that young person has diferent interests, a different vocabulary, a different thought world from that of his or her chronological peers. They are often shunned by their contemporaries, are considered teachers' pets, called "eggheads" or whatever the current slang expression is for those who are very bright. As one gifted girl said, "It's bad enough to be taller than the boys, but when you're smarter, too, it's fatal."

Anything that makes persons feel different makes them feel inferior—so we have the strange phenomenon of gifted children feeling inferior or inadequate. Some even fake "down" on tests, just to be one of the group.

This group has been largely neglected by the church. The literature on religious education and pastoral counseling hardly touches on their needs at all.

I had a unique experience a few years ago when I wrote a little book entitled *The Church: The Gifted and Retarded Child* (Bethany Press, 1957). After this book came out, I was invited to make many speeches on the church and the retarded child, even to the White House Conference on Children and Youth. Only one group ever asked me to speak on the church and the gifted child. Just one. The Department of Religious Education of Southwestern Baptist Theological School asked me to speak on the religious education of the gifted. No one ever asked me to speak on counseling with the gifted.

When I was asked to speak on the retarded, I often did so by contrasting them with the gifted. Thus I managed to get across my concern for both groups.

At the other end of the scale is this other group, similar in numbers but almost completely opposite in some areas of need. They are not in advance of those in their chronological age group; they are a few years behind. The more severe ones may be in training schools where they are receiving special care, but many are in the community, often in special education classes, or in regular classes, struggling to keep up. All of them, except the ones in institutions, may be in the congregation. All their families may be in the congregation also. Sometimes the family needs a ministry more than does the retarded person.

In working in this area, one of the first things I want to do is be sure the diagnosis is correct. There have been all too many cases where people have been thought retarded but actually were not. I know of one situation where a child was considered retarded but actually was deaf. The parents didn't know it, his teachers didn't know it, but when his deafness was discovered he proved to be quite capable of functioning in a normal manner. I recall another situation when doing graduate work at the University of Nebraska. A child who had been ill from early childhood with asthma and other complications was referred to the educational clinic for evaluation. He looked retarded; he acted retarded; his doctor thought he might be retarded. He was assigned to me. It was suggested that I should start by giving him the Stanford-Binet test of mental ablity. He scored an IQ of 122. I can even remember the exact score, I was so surprised. One thing for sure, he was not retarded. A high score is always reassuring. You can't answer the questions if you can't understand them.

A low test should always be rechecked, but a high score is very comforting. I could say with certainty he was above average in mental ability. He still had problems. He had never played as other children had played. He was socially retarded. He still had physical problems, but he was not mentally retarded.

I would like to turn now to the comparison and contrast of these two groups of exceptional people. Physically there is a marked contrast. The very thorough research of Lewis Terman and his associates at Stanford University reveals very clearly that the gifted have better health, stronger physiques than the general population, let alone the retarded. The retarded, on the other hand, have more illnesses, more physical handicaps than the general population.

Socially, we have already indicated that both groups have problems but for different reasons. Both tend to be shunned by their playmates on the playground; both have difficulty finding companions who share the same interests; both tend to be left out of social groups. There are obvious exceptions to this, but it occurs often enough to be considered a common problem. Not to feel accepted by our peers has definite emotional overtones.

Educationally, both groups have problems but again for different reasons. For the gifted, school is too easy; they are bored. They are not challenged and may tend to develop poor study habits, which become a handicap in college or graduate school. They may tend to look down on others who find school difficult, which only increases the isolation and alienation mentioned above. The retarded, on the other hand, find school too difficult; they cannot keep up; they are under constant stress; they never get good grades, which are such a mark of achievement in our culture. They have the same need for a sense of achievement, recognition, and acceptance that any other children have, but they are so often denied any of the things that secure it. They are never on the honor roll, never get elected to office, never make the team—all the things that give prestige in our society.

Religiously, the gifted ask the basic existential and theological questions when they are several years younger than the average person. Perhaps the church school teacher or the parent cannot answer them, so they say, "Go see the pastor." If the pastor is too busy or makes light of the request, the child gets the feeling that adults don't know the answers or that it is wrong to ask. William Ellery Channing, prominent New England preacher in Colonial America, as a boy, once wrote in his diary, "I can find no one with whom I can discuss spiritual matters. I am forced to confine my thoughts to my own bosom." What a pity. I doubt that such an experience was confined to Colonial New England.

The retarded, on the other hand, do not even understand the questions their more gifted friends may ask. They cannot do abstract reasoning. They are confused by it all. Yet they do respond to religious music; they can be taught to pray. They do have a feeling of the presence of God, and they can respond to simple religious and moral teaching.

Recognizing these groups' differences, I should hasten to point out that on a very deep level, all these children are the same. They all need to be loved and accepted. They all need to feel understood and cared for. They all need to experience worship and to know the meaning and value of prayer. They all need to have a pastor who understands them as persons and cares for them as individuals—one who will listen to them and treat them as persons, not as categories.

The pastor may have both these groups in the same

congregation. I can still recall a congregation where on any given Sunday morning, it was quite possible to have several Ph.D.s in the congregation; it was a church in a university community. At the same time, across the aisle, there could be persons who had spent their early lives in the state school for the retarded and were now living in the same community. They may have been holding the hymnbook upside down, but they were in church and they were enjoying the music. They came to church from very different backgrounds, with different interests, different vocabularies, different abilities to understand, but they heard the same sermon.

This does not mean that the pastor should be overawed by the presence of the Ph.D.s or talk down to the slow learners. Richard Baxter used to preach a sermon once a year that was over the heads of the congregation, just to show them what he could do every Sunday if he had to. This is not what the gifted person needs or wants. The gifted person will be more impressed by a sermon that is simple and sincere. After all, how many big words do you find in the parables of Jesus? Retarded persons may not understand all of a sermon but they do enjoy being in worship. They can respond to the music; they appreciate feeling that they belong and are accepted. And that is a task both for the pastor and for the entire congregation.

We haven't discussed counseling methods or techniques. Obviously they will vary with the mental abilities of the person being counseled. The gifted can come to insights quickly; they respond to more insight-oriented types of counseling. The retarded need more behaviorally oriented guidance and, at times, simple instruction. Both need the assurance that the pastor genuinely understands and cares—which, after all, is the heart of all pastoral counseling.

## · E I G H T ·

# Pastoral Counseling with the Rich and the Poor

I was raised in a middle-class home, went to a middle-class church, attended a middle-class school. Most of my friends were, and still are, middle-class people. This is also true of many Protestant pastors. Does this mean that the pastor who has a middle-class background is disqualified for counseling with the rich or the poor?

The answer is no. What it does mean is that the pastor must recognize that in counseling with the rich or the poor, he or she is dealing with people from different parts of town whose lives are shaped by very different cultural patterns and environmental forces. Michael Harrington taught us a long time ago that there is a culture of poverty (*The Other America: Poverty in the United States,* Macmillan, 1962). There is also a culture of affluence. The differences are more than differences in the houses they live in. There is a difference in life-style. The pastor, therefore, must make a conscious effort to understand the varied life-styles that are often different from that of the pastor and the pastor's family.

I was asked by Abingdon Press to prepare two articles for their new dictionary on pastoral care. One was to be on counseling the affluent, one on counseling the poor. To prepare these two articles simultaneously was an interesting experience in contrasts.

In preparing the material on the rich, I consulted three sources. First was the New Testament; second was a group of pastors who had experience in serving wealthy congregations and who had demonstrated real pastoral skills; and third was my own observation and experience in counseling with wealthy persons.

The New Testament's most frequent mentions of riches are in the form of warnings. Jesus spoke often of the peril of riches. "And Jesus looked around and said to his disciples, 'How hard it will be for those who have riches to enter the kingdom of God'" (Mark 10:23). Again, "What does it profit a man, to gain the whole world and forfeit his life?" (Mark 8:36). Again, "Take heed, and beware of all covetousness; for a man's life does not consist in the abundance of his possessions" (Luke 12:15). "Do not lay up for yourselves treasures on earth, where moth and rust consume and where thieves break in and steal, but lay up for yourselves treasures in heaven. . . . For where your treasure is, there will your heart be also" (Matt. 6:19-21).

It was the danger of worshiping wealth of which Jesus spoke. Jesus often visited in the homes of the wealthy. He advised one rich young ruler to sell what he had and give to the poor. He didn't demand that of Nicodemus or Zacchaeus. When wealth is worshiped, it becomes idolatry.

Pastors who work with the wealthy point out that rich people often have a feeling of being used. They are suspicious of friendships because they feel so many approach them only for their money, for what they can do for them. One pastor who has served wealthy congregations in the Midwest and the Southwest said, "Their affluence gives them a distorted sense of reality, a distorted sense of self. They have the dilemma of being powerful." This brings to mind the oft-quoted statement, "Power tends to corrupt; absolute power corrupts absolutely." This is very different from the problems of the poor. Theirs is the other side of the coin—they are powerless. Both power and powerlessness create problems.

The wealthy are often envied by other people. This envy may be sensed consciously or unconsciously, and it leads to a feeling of alienation, even of loneliness. One pastor said, "It is lonely at the top." Another said, "They have no more worlds to conquer." As one wealthy woman said to her psychiatrist, "If you could just convince me my life had some meaning, you wouldn't be hearing this silly story about my nerves."

My own observation and somewhat limited experience in dealing with the rich is that basically they are just like everyone else—they have the same feelings of guilt and anxiety, even of inadequacy. They have the same need to be understood and loved, the same need for courage and faith. None of these can be purchased for any amount of money.

Just as they share the same needs and concerns, the wealthy also have problems that are unique to their situation. Their affluence affects how they look at life, at others, and how others look at them. It is a false assumption that the luxuries and advantages that go with material success and social prestige always provide satisfaction and contentment.

If we could draw an imaginary line down through society and place on one side all those who find life challenging and worthwhile, and on the other side all who find life futile and meaningless, we would find that not all the wealthy would be on the meaningful side of the line—far from it. The opposite is also true. Not all the poor would be on the meaningless or frustrated side of the line either. Some of the most creative, victorious lives in history rose from the ranks of poverty—Charles Dickens, Abraham Lincoln, George Frederick Handel, Marie Curie, Ralph Waldo Emerson, to name a few.

Let's go now across town to the group at the lower end of the economic scale. We are speaking now of far greater numbers. We are thinking now of 15 to 20 percent of the total population—or millions of people. These figures, staggering as they are, do not tell the whole story. There are many more whom Harrington describes as "just the other side of poverty." While they are not officially counted as poor, they share all the concerns, frustrations, and feelings of the poor because they still exist at levels below what is necessary for common decency.

The Bible has much to say about these people, also. The first line of the Forty-first Psalm reads, "Blessed is he who considers the poor." Throughout both the Old and New Testaments, there are numerous admonitions to consider and care for the poor. It was an integral part of the Old Testament law; it was central in the preaching of the prophets; it was at the heart of Jesus' message of love and compassion. The parable of the good Samaritan implies that anyone who is facing misfortune or need is our neighbor and should be the subject of our concern. In the parable of the last judgment in the twenty-fifth chapter of Matthew, Jesus listed the righteous as those who had fed the hungry, clothed the naked, visited the sick and imprisoned, and then he said, "As you did it to one of the least of these my brethren, you did it to me" (Matt. 25:40).

A long time ago William Pitt said, "Poverty is no disgrace, but it is damned annoying." In America it can be both annoying and a disgrace. One thing that is different today from Pitt's day or any previous generation, is that poverty is surrounded by so much affluence. While poverty has created a major problem for a large segment of society, the majority are enjoying luxuries that are unequaled in any previous generation.

Many of these who are poor are unchurched. In fact, one characteristic of the culture of poverty is that the poor do not belong to anything. Furthermore, they have the feeling that the rest of society, including the church, does not care. This is not fair to some pastors or to some churches, but there is enough truth in it to cause some soul searching. If they did attend the average middle-class church, would they be made to feel at home?

When I was directing the Pastoral Care Center at the Divinity School at Texas Christian University, we conducted a program of pastoral care in a poverty area of Fort Worth for twelve years. We learned many things—the first being that we didn't know much about counseling with the poor. When we started the program, there were many who were skeptical and some who were opposed to such a venture. They said that a person with a middle-class background cannot understand the problems of the poor and will not be accepted by them. We soon found that there were reasons for such concerns and that we had to develop a whole new set of approaches. More depended on attitudes than upon methods, but our work could be done. It wasn't easy; we had to be satisfied with small gains, but things could be accomplished.

One of the first things we recognized was that there was a real language gap. The poor have two languages—the middle class only have one. Some call it ghettoese; some call it street talk; some call it the hidden language of the poor. We found over two hundred words that have different meanings in different parts of town. A "pig" is an animal in suburbia; it is a police officer in the ghetto. A "working girl" is an employed young woman in suburbia; she is a prostitute in the ghetto. Mother's Day is a special Sunday in suburbia; it is the day the welfare check comes in the ghetto. The poor would much prefer that middle-class pastors stick to the language they know best and not try to use terms that are not familiar to them. When they attempt to do so, they only look foolish in the eyes of the poor.

A major difference we found between the poor and the people in suburbia was that the poor almost always had economic problems that overshadowed their personal problems. In working with the affluent, you seldom have problems with how to pay the rent, how to apply for food stamps, how to get a job, how to afford the doctor or the dentist. These things are taken for granted. With the poor, these problems are daily concerns that must be faced before they can get down to talking about other more psychological or emotional feelings. Their problems have to do with jobs, food, clothing, transportation, rent, medical and dental care. The pastor who would work with the poor must be half social worker and thoroughly familiar with community resources.

We also found that the methods must be altered. Modern psychotherapy, which has greatly influenced pastoral counseling, was predominantly a middle-class movement. It was designed for people who had previous association with other professionals—the family doctor, dentist, and lawyer. The poor have no such relationships. Their experience with professionals has often been standing in line, waiting their turn at the county hospital, or seeking free help at the legal aid society. Psychotherapy is also based on the premise that people want to verbalize their anxieties and concerns. The poor are not used to verbalization. They respond to more action-oriented approaches. They need to see some action, some change, some practical help.

Perhaps the biggest difference between the two groups is in the motivation or expectation of change. The poor have had no past, so they do not anticipate much in the future. They have never experienced success; they have not observed success in the community in which they live, so consequently, they do not expect it in the future. They have few role models to identify with, and some of those they do have are criminals.

Emotional problems that cause difficulty are basically the same for everyone, but for different reasons. Stress is one of the major concerns right now. Books are written about it; seminars are held about it; articles are published on it—all point out that a person can stand only so much stress. Among the poor, stress is always present. It is cyclical. Lack of funds means limited medical care and lack of education. Lack of education means limited employment. Limited employment means lack of funds. Among the poor the stress is always present. It is almost never relieved. As one man put it, "It is trying to make do with a string when a rope is needed."

All people feel inferior; with the poor it is intensified. Ben Bagdikian said, "Poverty invites comparison with others, and it is the comparison that produces the sense of failure" (*In the Midst of Plenty,* New American Library, 1964, p. 135). Anger is difficult to deal with in any part of town, but with the poor it is often deep, unresolved, and at times—explosive. No generalization should be applied to any group, yet many of the poor are angry and not without reason. They are the victims of injustice; they see the privileges and luxuries of others; they are forced to accept welfare or handouts, which make them feel dependent. It may be suppressed, even repressed, but their anger is there.

The pastor who attempts to counsel with people who are poor must be conscious of the reality and the power of such emotions. The pastor is also seen by many in the poverty area as representing a church that has exploited them, neglected them, and withdrawn from them. This does not say such counseling is impossible, but it is difficult. Much depends on the pastor's own attitudes. The pastor must avoid any semblance of patronage, any feeling of superiority, any sentimentality or piety. The poor are realists. They will see through any false humility or self-righteousness. The only way we can counsel with the poor is to be conscious of our own limitations, or, in other words, be humble. We must be patient, be satisfied with small gains. Recognize that obstacles are enormous. At the same time, we must be optimistic that some results can take place. We must be understanding and empathetic, but above all we should have genuine feelings of appreciation and respect for the poor.

Having said all this, I should emphasize that we have much to learn from the poor. Most of the studies of the poor stress their problems. Very little is said about their strengths. One reason is that most people who write about the poor are hoping to arouse concern or raise funds. This is best done by emphasizing deprivation, or as one man put it, stressing the "plight of the poor." We must recognize that the poor also have strengths. They have what are called survival techniques which people in a more affluent part of town know nothing about. They maintain a sense of humor that is contagious and inspiring. Most of all, many of them have a deep religious faith that is both simple and profound. We do have much to learn from them.

Whether the parish pastor is ministering to the very wealthy, or the very poor—it is a real challenge and an opportunity.

# The Parish Pastor as Marriage and Family Counselor

There are seven presuppositions on which I base my discussion of the parish pastor as a counselor in marriage and family matters. These are not open to debate. They have been established through extensive, far-reaching, experience.

1. Nothing is more sacred or significant than marriage and the home. I assume all pastors would agree with that.

2. Pastors will be consulted about marriage and family concerns more frequently than any other matter.

3. There is a vast amount of literature and other resources about marriage and the family to help the pastor understand this area. This is in contrast to some other topics discussed in this volume where resources are very limited.

4. Marriage and family life are in a great state of flux in our culture. Masculine and feminine roles, moral standards,

concepts of human sexuality, even the nature and place of marriage itself are in a constant state of confusion and transition.

5. All marriages, all families have some problems. Marriage is the most intimate, personal, complicated, permanent relationship in the world. It offers life's highest values and deepest satisfactions. Because of its complexity and the tensions and pressures of society as a whole, it is not surprising that problems arise. The big question is how such problems are resolved.

6. The extensive experience of marriage and family therapists, as well as that of psychologists, psychiatrists, and pastoral counselors, gives ample testimony that marriages can be helped, that people can improve their family life.

7. The parish pastor, because of the nature of the ministry and the other responsibilities a pastor carries, is in a unique position to serve as a marriage and family counselor. The pastor conducts weddings and therefore is identified with marriage from the beginning. Because the pastor preaches on love and understanding and is present in the home to share both joys and disappointments, it is quite natural that people think of a pastor when problems arise.

Besides these presuppositions, there are at least nine areas where a pastor has responsibilities that relate to marriage and the family. Three occur before marriage and six occur after.

1. Before marriage the pastor should povide *premarital education.* This can be done with groups, with couples, or with individuals. This counseling should cover all such matters as the sacredness of the marriage vows, human sexuality, family financing, relationship with in-laws, the meaning of parenting.

2. *Premarital guidance* goes one step further. It helps couples take the information provided by the pastor and apply it to their own lives. Information about family finances is one thing. Helping a couple determine a budget on a limited income is another, especially if they are in graduate school and have few resources. The same thing is true of other topics such as sexual adjustment, parenting, relating to in-laws, communication, or any other aspect of marriage.

3. *Premarital counseling* is more emotion-oriented than information-centered. Counseling and guidance overlap, but for purposes of discussion I separate them. Here are situations that are highly charged with emotion, such as when parents disapprove of the marriage, or in interfaith marriage when there is disagreement about what church to affiliate with, or when the bride is pregnant and the couple is not sure whether or not to get married, or there is difference of opinion about having children, or great differences in their ages. The list could go on and on. Here more than education and guidance is needed. Only counseling will suffice.

There are six areas of responsibility a pastor has in working with married couples.

1. First is *normal conflict*. I say *normal* because there is a certain amount of conflict in every situation. Once when a couple told George Buttrick they had never had an argument or a difference of opinion, he replied, "How horribly dull."

It has been pointed out that there is a difference in "constructive" and "destructive" conflict. Constructive conflict centers on the issue, not the person. It can lead to a closer and deeper relationship.

Destructive conflict centers on the person, not the issue. It hurts, it alienates, it destroys. One of the areas that is left out of most books on preparing for marriage is the art of quarreling. It is a real art.

2. The next area is *severe conflict*. The difference is more one of degree than of kind. There is a difference in intensity. The situation has become unbearable. It may include unfaithfulness, violent arguments, physical or verbal abuse. The couple already may have separated or sought the services of an attorney. In such situations, the pastor must bargain for some time to delay the legal action until some effort can be made to work on the problem. It may be that the pastor feels the problems are too time-consuming or complicated for pastoral counseling. The pastor must decide whether some of the violent behavior is symptomatic of a marriage problem or of a deeper emotional problem.

On some of these occasions the pastor's greatest service may be to refer the couple to the hands of someone who has the time and training to deal with their needs more effectively; then the pastor continues as a pastor, not as a therapist.

3. When the situation is such that the people feel that divorce is the only alternative, then the pastor serves as a *divorce counselor*. The pastor helps them work through the grief that usually follows a divorce, helps them make readjustments and develop enough understanding so that the mistakes of the past will not be repeated in the future.

4. There are many other relationships a pastor has with a family where they are dealing with deep personal *family concerns*. The family is not in conflict but may be perplexed, confused, uncertain. People often consult a pastor about such matters as: What should we do with our retarded child? Would it be better to place the child in a school for the

retarded or keep him or her at home? A husband may ask, Should I sell my business and go to seminary? I would like to, but my family isn't so sure. What should we do with our elderly parents? Again, the list goes on and on.

5. Of course there are the usual *pastoral care* responsibilities. The pastor ministers to families in time of sickness, trouble, and sorrow. The pastor also shares their joys, achievements, and successes.

6. The final, and often one of the most neglected areas, is *marriage enrichment*. This is what Howard Clinebell calls growth counseling.

The primary emphasis of both secular and pastoral counseling has been to take people at the neurotic or maladjusted level and help them get back to, or up to, the normal level. It is equally important to help people and families who are not maladjusted or neurotic but who could be functioning at a more creative, meaningful level. Helping people to grow is one of the real challenges of both pastoral counseling and marriage therapy.

When a pastor is functioning as a marriage and family counselor, the pastor, by and large, is working with normal people. He or she is not attempting deep psychotherapy. When psychotherapy is indicated, a referral should be considered. The pastor is dealing primarily with relationships—husband and wife, parent and child, couples and in-laws. The pastor is working as a pastor, not as a psychiatrist, not as a psychologist, not as an attorney, not as a judge—but as a pastor. As a pastor he or she uses all the skills of pastoral counseling, all the resources of the church, plus the powerful healing forces of Christian faith and Christian love.

There is no area of pastoral counseling that offers more variety, requires more skill and deeper understanding of life and human possibilities than marriage and family counseling. There are certain attitudes and behavior patterns that are common to most people who seek marriage counseling. The word *most* is an important one. Not all people have the same concerns or the same problems. Therefore, in the following list, I preface each statement with the words *usually* or *often*. Each statement presents a condition that many people have. Each statement includes a reference to the responsibilities and the opportunities a pastor has when presented with such situations.

1. There is usually a lack of information about the nature and meaning of marriage and the marriage relationship. Here the pastor is primarily an educator. The pastor teaches the meaning of marriage and how to attain lasting relationships.

2. There is usually a breakdown in communication, especially at the feeling level. In fact, real communication may never have existed. A pastor should be a specialist in communication skills. Teaching people to experience honest communication may be all that is needed.

3. There is usually an inability to solve mutual problems or to differ (or quarrel) in a nondestructive way. As stated earlier, teaching people the fine art of quarreling is a great service.

4. People are often unaware of how their words or actions, even their tone of voice, affect other people. Many are so wrapped up in their own hurts that they are insensitive to the hurts of others. If a pastor can help people develop a sensitivity to the feelings of others, it can do much to relieve pain and restore broken relationships.

5. There is usually a nonsupportive relationship between members of a family and an inability to sense or meet the emotional needs of others. Helping people to provide support, reassurance, and encouragement to each other can change the whole atmosphere of a relationship.

6. There is often a lot of anger ranging from mild irritation to vindictiveness and bitterness. Unresolved or uncontrolled anger is destructive both to the one who has it and the one against whom it is directed. The pastor's task is to help people drain off their anger, to understand the causes of their anger, to be aware of the negative results of anger, to reduce and control their anger so that it is not destructive or alienating.

7. There is often a rather intense spirit of competition, not dissimilar to the sibling rivalry found in children. Helping people to mature and replace competition with cooperation can reduce a lot of unnecessary tension and conflict.

8. There is usually, though not always, an unsatisfactory physical relationship, and an unawareness of the meaning of human sexuality. The pastor is not a sex therapist, but the pastor can relieve a lot of unnecessary guilt and anxiety and can interpret the Christian and the biblical view of sex.

9. There is often, though not always, tension concerning money, how it is secured, how it is divided, and how it is spent. A pastor is not a financial adviser but can do much to help people work through their financial concerns and conflicts together and at the same time attain a sense of Christian stewardship.

10. There is often, though not always, tension concerning vocational decisions and goals, and the way vocation impinges on family life. This was dealt with in an earlier chapter.

11.  In some cases, the problem is cultural as much as it is interpersonal. There is too much to do, too little time to do it, too many activities, too-crowded schedules—all of which result in fatigue, stress, and no time to be together. It is a logistical problem as well as an interpersonal one. The pastor can help people establish priorities, manage their time, and transcend cultural pressures.

12.  There is often a feeling of surprise or unreality. "This can't be happening to us." The pastor provides reassurance that some conflicts are normal, that most of them can be worked through.

13.  There is usually a sense of urgency, a desire to get problems solved quickly and get back to normal. The pastor must teach the value of patience and help people realize that complicated issues of long standing take time to work through. Problems that have developed over years cannot be resolved in minutes, even in hours.

14.  The general atmosphere is usually discouraged and pessimistic. There is often a grief reaction, due to a loss in the relationship or the anticipation of a loss—it doesn't matter which. The pastor helps them understand what is taking place, stands by them in the experience, and helps them attain a new sense of optimism and hope.

15.  There is often a feeling of having been misunderstood, mistreated, even deceived or betrayed. In some cases, this deceit has occurred. The sense of alienation may be very real. While such behavior must be dealt with and some assurance given that it will not be repeated, the pastor also is a minister of reconciliation. One of a pastor's most difficult tasks is to help people give and receive the grace of forgiveness.

16. There is very seldom any common bond of worship or a commitment to faith. Here, again, the pastor is a specialist. The pastor helps the couple to view both their relationship and their lives from the perspective of faith and to share in experiences of worship, fellowship, and service with the church. It is a spirit of faith and trust that provides the foundations of the home.

These are some of the general areas where a pastor must be expected to provide a ministry. There may be others, but these are enough to present both a challenge and great opportunities to any pastor who is concerned about the families within the parish.

# The Parish Pastor as Spiritual Director

Some time ago I received in the mail some publicity material from a Catholic university announcing a new program at the master's level in spiritual direction and counseling. I do not know how the program has developed, but the idea has significant implications for the parish pastor.

Such a program presents intriguing possibilities and at the same time points up an area that has been largely neglected in the literature on pastoral counseling and also by many pastors. Those in traditional Protestant churches have much to learn from our Catholic and Anglican friends at this point.

Men like Charles Whiston and Morton Kelsey strongly claim that anyone who is serious about the spiritual life would benefit from a good spiritual director. They are not talking about a counselor or a confessor, although at times the spiritual director may be called upon to counsel or to hear a person make a confession. They are talking about a guide, a teacher, or a director. They are thinking of something that must be done on an individual basis. While certain general principles apply, each person's needs and background are different—each person must be guided in an individual way.

The purpose of such a director is to explain why we need the spiritual life and suggest how we could go about maintaining such a life. Much of his or her work is very practical, focusing on such areas as prayer and meditation, private devotion, public worship, inspirational and devotional reading, scripture, religious faith, and a life of trust, and commitment.

The spiritual director provides an opportunity to discuss such matters. He or she can explain, interpret, instruct, or clarify.

At times, the director may offer support and encouragement when a person loses interest or becomes discouraged. On other occasions, the director examines a person, like a wise teacher who uses questions and reviews to foster growth. The director always will require discipline and continued effort.

The director is a specialist in religious experience and helps individuals grow in both their understanding and application of religion. (See Whiston, *Instructions in the Life of Prayer*, Forward Movement Publications, 1972, and Kelsey, *The Other Side of Silence*, Paulist Press, 1976).

People are hungry for this kind of guidance. A young professional man, active in the church, said, "I go to church, I always have. I own a Bible, but I never read it. There's got to be more to religion than I am getting." A young mother said, "Could you suggest a good book on prayer? I need to know more about prayer." A regular in church attendance asked, "Could you recommend some books on faith and the religious life?" The clergy are not exempt. A young pastor said, "I don't need counseling as such. I'm not upset or anxious. I want to know how to get more out of prayer and worship. It's hard to conduct worship while worshiping at the same time. My personal devotional life is almost nonexistent."

These aren't exact quotes, but they represent real people. Any pastor could add dozens of such statements. Perhaps one of the reasons for the popularity of such practices as transcendental meditation, yoga, and the widespread interest in Eastern religions is a lack of spiritual direction and guidance in many of our Protestant churches.

There are some differences between spiritual direction and the subjects discussed in other chapters. A. Graham Ikin, who also advocates spiritual direction, compares this difference to the time when she was teaching a well-known church dignitary to paddle a canoe. He first zigzagged from one bank to another until he began to understand her instructions about inserting the blade in the water and moving forward on his chosen path. Many people can learn how to progress in the spiritual life if there is someone to guide them. But they have to paddle their own canoe! Ikin also points out that there are differences, not only in the procedures, but also in the way the spiritual director views the people with whom he or she is working. While psychotherapists speak of their people as patients or clients, spiritual directors view their people as pupils or students (Ikin, *New Concepts in Healing,* Association Press, 1965, p. 44).

There is another difference between this discussion and other topics in this study. When I discussed earlier what we can learn from the psychologists and psychotherapists, I was describing an area that is relatively new and in a constant state of flux. New ideas, new procedures, new schools of thought constantly emerge. It is all counselors can do to keep abreast of the most recent developments. Books that are important this year are out of date in ten years, if not sooner.

In thinking of spiritual disciplines, I think of things that are very old—as old as the book of Psalms, the *Confessions* of Saint Augustine, Loyola's *Spiritual Exercises,* or other medieval handbooks and devotional guides. This does not mean contemporary publications don't have value. It means we must think in terms of both thoughts and procedures that have proven effective for centuries. There are no new developments that will replace Thomas à Kempis' *Imitation of Christ,* or Brother Laurence's *Practice of the Presence of God.*

Psychotherapeutic methods are effective because they enable persons to make use of their own inner strengths, their drive toward maturity, their capacity for self-understanding and healthy interpersonal relationships. Without these capacities, no form of psychotherapy would be effective.

Religious or spiritual resources produce meaningful results because people also have the capacity to respond to spiritual realities.

Harry Emerson Fosdick gave a series of lectures in the difficult and confusing 1950s. His lectures were published under the title *A Faith for Tough Times.* He expressed the conviction that "the human soul at its best experiences invading spiritual forces which can transform, illumine, direct, and empower life."

This is true, he said, because:

1. Persons have an inborn capacity to be inspired.
2. Persons have an inborn capacity for worship.
3. Persons have an inborn capacity for spiritual companionship.
4. Persons have an inborn capacity to experience transforming invasions of power that make life all over.
5. Persons have an inborn capacity to be a channel of spiritual dynamic from beyond themselves.

Fosdick says, "Just as around our bodies is a physical world from which we draw out physical strength, so around our spirits is a Spiritual Environment, with which we can live in vital contact and from which all can draw replenishing power. He who understands that has entered into the profoundest experience of the Christian life" (Fosdick, *A Faith for Tough Times,* Harper & Brothers, 1952, pp. 96-99).

It is because these things are natural to human experience that religious resources are not only appropriate but at times the method of choice. The popularity of counseling and psychotherapy has resulted in many pastors developing skills in psychotherapeutic techniques and neglecting traditional church-oriented religious resources.

Paul Pruyser of the Menninger Clinic says, "It seems to me that pastors should not overlook their unique resources in counseling. Scripture readings, prescribed meditation on well-chosen biblical themes between sessions, prayer, and quasi-sacramental gestures such as benedictions . . .should not be discarded out of fear that they are *ipso facto* contradicting to psychological counseling technique" (Pruyser, "Use and Neglect of Pastoral Resources," *Pastoral Psychology,* September 1972, p. 12).

The parish pastor, as Pruyser points out, is uniquely qualified for such a ministry. We do not have space to discuss all the possibilities of spiritual directions but will refer to three of the oldest, most familiar of the spiritual resources: biblical meditation, private prayer, and devotional literature.

It is not being critical to say that there is a great amount of biblical illiteracy in the Protestant church. With some people, the pastor must begin with the simplest instruction and interpretation. There are occasions when a pastor has to correct biblical misinterpretation. The Bible, like all powerful things, can be used in an unhealthy way. Some Bible study and instruction may be necessary before it can be used as a spiritual discipline.

The Bible can be studied as literature; it can be studied historically and biographically; it can be studied critically and theologically. All this study is valid and should be an important part of any program of biblical study. In this discussion, however, I am thinking of using the Bible as a basis of meditation.

Meditation is probably the world's oldest religious exercise, found in most of the world's ancient religions. It was in Hinduism, Buddhism, all forms of mysticism, medieval handbooks for monasteries. The Bible is full of it. The book of Psalms refers to meditating in the night watches and perhaps the most familiar prayer in the entire Old Testament states, "Let the words of my mouth and the meditation of my heart be acceptable in thy sight, O Lord, my rock and my redeemer" (Ps. 19:14).

A few years ago Herbert Benson, a Boston physician, made a study of hypertension. He evaluated everything from tranquilizers to transcendental meditation and came to the conclusion that the one most effective method of counteracting tension was meditation. He included these findings in a book entitled *The Relaxation Response* (William Morrow, 1975), which was on the best seller lists for several months. Perhaps the popularity of this book is one indication of the widespread hunger for something that can reduce the pressures and tensions of modern life.

The principles Benson advocated were quite simple. They required only four things: a quiet place, a comfortable position, a passive attitude, and a center of focus. I talked to Dr. Benson about this and asked him why the Scripture couldn't be a good center of focus. He said it could, as long as it was just one verse.

In Benson's thinking, it didn't matter too much what the focus was, as long as it was in the context of the other three principles and was done regularly over a period of time.

There have been many empirical studies that verify Benson's findings—meditation does have a quieting, calming effect and often leads to insight and even improved health. This is apparently true of all forms of meditation.

More recently, Dr. Benson has written a second book, *Beyond the Relaxation Response.* In this book he reaffirms his former findings of the value of meditation but adds another very important dimension called the Faith Factor. Meditation has even greater value when our meditation is centered on the reality of faith (see Benson, *Beyond the Relaxation Response,* Times Books, 1983).

The difference between Christian meditation and other forms is the object of focus. In the Christian, the object of focus is a biblical truth, especially the life and teachings of Jesus. This was the central theme of Ignatius Loyola's *Spiritual Exercises* written a long time ago for the guidance of those in the monastery, who were instructed to meditate daily on scenes from the Passion Week. Centuries later, Leslie Weatherhead in the twentieth century advocated the same thing. He encouraged people to focus on scenes from the Gospels, to enter in imagination into the very experience of Jesus and his followers.

The Bible is the source book of the Christian faith. Its message has brought courage, hope, faith, and trust to millions. This has been demonstrated and documented again and again.

People can be led to use the Bible as a source of meditation and prayer. The procedures are simple. (1) They select a quiet place, free from interruptions and distractions; (2) They return to this place regularly and persistently; (3) The parishioners select a passage (or passages) that has meaning for them—a passage which, as the Quakers say, "speaks to their condition." The pastor can offer valuable help in the selection of these passages. (4) The parishioners ponder the passage, meditate on it, quietly, slowly consider its meaning and value. (5) They pray about it. It has been said we never really understand the Bible until we pray our way through it. (6) They apply it, live by it, make it an adventure of faith and life.

Another ancient spiritual resource is private prayer. There are frequent occasions when prayer or the devotional life may be a part of a discussion about some other problem. A parishioner may say, "I've prayed, but it doesn't seem to do any good," or "God doesn't hear me anymore." Such statements and a person's feelings about them should be seen as a part of the counseling process.

There are persons who sincerely want to explore, deepen, and enrich their prayer and devotional life. This is the group we have in mind here. This is spiritual direction.

This is one of those places where preaching and individual work overlap. Good preaching can help people understand prayer. The criticism sometimes voiced by laypersons is that preachers say they "ought" to pray. They don't say how.

Small groups, study groups, prayer groups are also valuable.

People can be helped by reading about prayer. There are many excellent books on prayer. There are some fine collections of books of prayers. Reading the prayers of others can be a guide and a stimulus to prayer. Such prayers do not take the place of the person's own prayers, but they are a valuable aid and can create the mood for prayer.

Reading alone, valuable as that is, is not enough. John R. Mott said that as a young man he was troubled about prayer and followed the same procedure he did in investigating all other matters. He went to the library and checked out all the books he could find on prayer. I think it was more than fifty volumes. This no doubt had real value, but when he finally closed the books and began to pray, he felt results.

So the pastor helps people learn about prayer and also how to pray. There are a few principles to follow.

The pastor must recognize that everyone must pray in his or her own way. Some pray most effectively in the morning, some in the evening. Some pray standing, some kneeling, some lying down. Muriel Lester said she prayed most effectively while walking, and Alan Knight Chalmers contended that he prayed when riding the New York subway. That is difficult to understand, but I'm sure it had meaning for him. What is natural for one may not be for another.

Prayer should include a wide range of personal and spiritual needs and experiences. There should be prayers of:

> adoration and praise
> gratitude and thanksgiving
> penitence and confession
> intercession and caring
> petition and aspiration
> dedication and commitment
> contemplation and receptivity

The two primary factors are sincerity and faith. We pray for faith. We pray in faith.

Prayer and Scripture are combined in devotional literature, plus the thoughts of a religious leader or a group of leaders. Devotional literature has proven its value for many centuries.

In psychotherapeutic terms, reading is referred to as *bibliotherapy,* which is the technical term meaning "healing by the printed word." Writers of books for psychotherapists are not familiar with devotional literature, which is seen as the province of the pastor. The pastor, therefore, can provide a special form of bibliotherapy.

Devotional literature comes in two broad, general categories: the classics and contemporary materials prepared for present-day use. The classics consist of those devotional materials that have survived the centuries because they have met human and spiritual needs. Contemporary literature consists of daily guides, meditations, and books of prayers.

Whether the material that is used is classical or contemporary, people usually need to know how to use it. We do not read devotional material in the same manner or even in the same frame of mind that we read the newspaper, a novel, or an academic book.

1. We read devotional literature slowly. Some materials can be read rapidly; some printed material we skim because that is all the content warrants. Not so with devotional literature. It is read slowly, leisurely, and carefully.

2. Devotional material should be read repeatedly. Some material we read once and that is enough. With some that's too much. Devotional material should be returned to again and again. Douglas Steere, an authority on such matters, says that we should read a good devotional book at least three times and preferably five. Each time, as with Scripture, we derive new meaning.

3. We should read small sections at a time. This may not always be true, but usually we should read small portions daily. Devotional material is prepared to be read over a period of time, not at one sitting.

4. Devotional material should be read historically. The more we know of the author, the culture in which he or she lived, the generation in which he or she wrote, the more we will understand the nature and content of the material. We don't have to shut off our critical faculties or accept medieval theology to benefit from the meditations of someone in another time and another culture who lived very close to God.

5. Devotional literature should be read selectively. A wise man once said, "If I read this book, I can't read that book." As Douglas Steere puts it, the limitations of time indicate a "wise use of the veto." He suggests that since no one can read everything, people should discover a few "staples" and concentrate on them until they know them.

6. Devotional material should be read more as the basis of meditation than for information. The principles for this kind of meditation are the same as those discussed in the

section on biblical meditation. We should read and ponder, read and ponder.

7. Devotional literature is read as a stimulus to prayer and worship. It does not take the place of our own prayers; it creates the mood for prayer; it encourages trust in prayer; it guides in the content of prayer.

We have discussed only three basic and tested spiritual resources—biblical meditation, private prayer, and devotional literature. There are other important items, such as how to benefit from public worship, how to appreciate the sacraments, an understanding of religious symbolism, the use of imagery, or the making of individual retreats.

There are certain general principles that apply to spiritual direction. The first is that the parish pastor is in a natural position for such a ministry. If pastors are to perform such functions, they must familiarize themselves with devotional materials—past and present—the lives of the saints, and those to whom the spiritual life has been real. They must have made a thorough study of both Scripture and prayer. First of all, however, they must give special attention to their own spiritual lives and discipline. This does not mean they have to attain perfection in order to direct others. It does mean that they must be committed to personal discipline and spiritual growth.

Both pastor and people need to recognize that it takes time and effort, patience and discipline, to develop a real devotional life. Some may be so naturally spiritual that this isn't necessary, but they are the exception.

Spiritual disciplines such as prayer, meditation, and worship must be pursued over a period of months and years. Occasional or sporadic attempts have little, if any, value. In psychological counseling, a person may come to an insight that clarifies a situation, and that takes care of it from then on. Not so in spiritual disciplines. They must be continued faithfully and patiently for long periods of time—for a lifetime, as a matter of fact.

Methods and procedures will change over the years. As our experience deepens, our understanding grows. As settings change and new materials become available, so the pattern of a person's devotional life changes, which is as it should be.

What appeals to us may not to another. William James reminded us a long time ago that there are "varieties of religious experience." The task of the director is to help the person find those things that have the most meaning for him or her.

The setting may do much to create a spirit of prayer and worship. Some prefer a view of nature, some a chapel or a sanctuary, some a picture or place in the home that suggests a religious theme. Religious symbols help create a spirit of reverence and devotion.

No one has a sense of reality in the spiritual life all the time. All the saints had what they called their "dry periods." Brother Laurence said he spent ten years before he felt his prayers got beyond the ceiling. It is when the dry periods occur that people must be helped to persist.

Spiritual disciplines must be related to other activities. Only those who also are committed to lives of activity and service can explore the depths of prayer and worship.

There is one more value derived from this form of ministry. The pastor who accepts the responsibility and the privilege of guiding others in a deeper understanding of the spiritual life will amost inevitably deepen his or her own.

# Preaching and Pastoral Counseling:

## Mutual Allies

Once while traveling in Scotland on a golf tour, I arrived in the ancient city of St. Andrews, known as the home of golf. When Sunday came, I looked around for a church to attend, as I always do. I wanted to go to a Church of Scotland, for I had long heard of their tradition of good biblical and theological preaching.

There was a small church within walking distance of the hotel. At the hour for the service to begin, the pastor, an elderly gentleman in a long black robe, with a white flowing beard—who looked for all the world like John Knox himself—started slowly down the center aisle of the church with a big pulpit Bible under his left arm and a shepherd's staff in his right hand.

He ascended the pulpit, placed the shepherd's staff in the corner, placed the Bible on the pulpit, and opened it to the lesson.

I thought, what a beautiful symbolism of that pastor's two main responsibilities. The Bible symbolized the prophetic ministry; the shepherd's staff symbolized the pastoral ministry. Granted that at times the two responsibilities may come into tension—on occasion be in conflict—but they should not be seen as two roles, but two functions of the same role—that is, to minister to the people in whatever way is most helpful. At times, a pastor can help the people most by preparing a well-thought-out interpretation of the gospel and applying it to life. At other times, the pastor may render the greatest service by listening to their deepest concerns and problems, one at a time.

I do not see these two functions as adversaries but as allies. Regrettably, not all people see it this way. As one preacher said, "I'm too busy to be concerned about people's individual problems." Many in the counseling field discount the value of preaching, and some of the psychotherapists aren't familiar with it at all.

For example, several years ago a well-trained and competent psychotherapist was visiting the seminary where I was teaching. It was my responsibility and privilege to introduce him to the various faculty members. When we met our professor of homiletics, I called him by name and said, "This is our homiletics man."

Later when we were by ourselves he said, "What is homiletics?"

I said, "It is the art of preaching."

He said, "I didn't know what it was, but I thought I could cure it if he would cooperate."

People smile when I recount this incident, and I do too, but it isn't really funny. It reflects an almost total lack of understanding of preaching and worship as one of the healing forces in life.

The pastor has one resource that is unique in all the helping professions—the sermon. Of all the counselors in the community, the pastor is the only one who appears before his or her counselees once a week and discusses the issues of life, proclaims a message, bears witness to a faith.

While the sermon is not often referred to as a counseling technique—and indeed, I do not think it should be—yet it is certainly a part of the pastoral task. As Charles Jefferson said a long time ago, "The minister does not cease to be a pastor when he enters the pulpit, rather he takes up one of the pastor's most exacting tasks" (Jefferson, *The Minister as Shepherd,* Crowell, 1912, p. 78).

Some have called this "life situation preaching." Wayne Oates refers to it as "therapeutic preaching." I prefer "pastoral preaching."

Pastoral work and preaching go together; each one can strengthen and help the other. Through the centuries, great pastors have sensed the relationship between preaching and the needs of their people. Horace Bushnell's great sermon "On the Dissolving of Doubt" grew out of his own struggle with doubt. A visitor to Trinity Church in Boston was asked what impressed him about Phillips Brooks' preaching and he said, "His obvious love for his people."

When Peter Ainslee was ministering to the Christian Temple in Baltimore, he said on those occasions when he was having difficulty in the preparation of a sermon he would put on his hat, make a round of pastoral calls and come back with "messages seething through his brain."

Since the advent of the pastoral counseling movement, there has been a tendency to downgrade the sermon as a real life-changing experience. This was not true of such men as Bushnell, Brooks, or Fosdick. In fact, Fosdick said he conceived of preaching as one form of counseling on a large scale.

Pastoral counseling and pastoral care contribute to each other in many ways. Pastoral work provides the background from which real preaching can come. Rufus Jones once said, "It is impossible to help a man with a message, unless you are willing to share his life." You can't know what these needs are unless you go where the people are or listen to them when they come to you.

Harry Emerson Fosdick early in his ministry wrote an article in *Harper's Magazine* entitled "What's the Matter with Preaching?" He felt the main problem with preaching was that it was not relevant enough to people's real-life concerns. "Every sermon," he said, "should have for its main business the solving of some problem—a vital, important problem, puzzling minds, burdening consciences, distracting lives. . . . One way or another they [the people in the congregation] should see that he is engaged in a serious and practical endeavor to state fairly a problem which actually exists in their lives and then to throw what light on it he can" (*Harper's Magazine,* July 1928).

Twenty-four years later, after his retirement, Fosdick wrote an article in another magazine and expressed the same philosophy, "Every sermon should have as its main business the head-on constructive meeting of some problem which is puzzling minds, burdening consciences, distracting lives, and no sermon which so meets real human difficulty, with light to throw on it and power to win victory over it, can possibly be futile" (*Pastoral Psychology,* 1952).

Pastoral work contributes to preaching in that it establishes a relationship between pastors and people. If the preachers have been faithful to their people as pastors, if they have been present and understanding in time of need, the people will listen to them with a new earnestness and receptivity when they get up to preach. Then, pastors are no longer just voices, professional speakers (preachers), but friends who have shared their lives. Homiletically, these pastors may not be powerful, but what they say will be heard.

The opposite is also true. If they show little or no concern in time of need, they may be homiletically perfect and present their sermons with a good delivery. But they will just be voices that are hired to preach.

Preaching also contributes to counseling in that through the sermon pastors establish their identities. If pastors speak as those who understand, as those who share the common struggles of all humankind, as those who care and offer hope—people will seek those pastors out. In fact, Dr. Fosdick once went so far as to say the test of a sermon was the number of people who wanted to discuss it with the pastor afterward.

Again, the opposite is also true. If the preaching is too judgmental, too sentimental, and oversimplified, people will feel that this pastor is not one who would understand.

In one study of people's problems and where they went for help, one person said, "Our pastor is a good man and he lives a good life, but I know he doesn't really know how I feel about not knowing what to do. If he really had to live the way we do, he'd understand better. . . . He doesn't know what life's problems are. How can he help?"

Preaching provides a background for counseling. When we go to a professional counselor, we don't know the therapist's background or philosophy. Preachers present the background of their thinking every week. Preachers/ pastors proclaim a message, express a philosophy of life. For many, this can be a form of preventive counseling. If preachers speak with real understanding, they can help people develop attitudes that help them to avoid problems and give them courage and faith.

There are some dangers that preachers must avoid. They should never use illustrations from their counseling in sermons. Even though the people being discussed may not be present, others may feel that the preacher could just as easily talk about them in public.

Preachers should not make sermons a running account of psycholgical problems in theological settings. Preaching should include all areas of the Christian faith.

Preachers should not oversimplify and try to do in one sermon what would need hours of counseling. It is one thing to preach on guilt; it is another to hear a person make a lengthy confession and help him or her realize the fact of forgiveness and walk in newness of life.

In fact, pastors have no right to raise deep emotional problems from the pulpit unless they are willing to spend time with persons in private.

Finally, preaching has and does produce results—real results. This has been demonstrated over and over again.

In his autobiography, William Grenfell tells how he wandered into a meeting where Dwight L. Moody was preaching and was so challenged to a life of service that his whole life was changed. Barton W. Stone, pioneer leader of the Disciples of Christ, said his whole outlook was changed by a sermon entitled "God Is Love." He had been a believer for a long time, but that sermon did something that brought all things together for him, giving him faith. John R. Mott, while a student at Cornell University, went to a service in the University Chapel when a preacher from England was preaching. Mott went reluctantly, but he stayed to be inspired. The preacher, whose name was C. T. Studd, seemed to be speaking directly to him. His theme was, "Seekest thou great things for thyself, seek them not; seek first the Kingdom of God." This so impressed young Mott that he sought out the Reverend Mr. Studd after the service, and they had a long and profitable conversation. That night Mott made what he called his "life investment decision." The rest is history.

It was a good sermon that awakened him to possibilities. It was a preacher's willingness to talk with him as an individual that led to a commitment, so preaching and counseling were combined—as allies.

I agree that these are dramatic illustrations. In the majority of cases, results are more gradual and imperceptible. We should never discount the accumulative influence of good preaching over a period of time. As a member of Phillips Brooks' congregation put it, "He always makes me feel so strong."

Perhaps one more thing about preaching that makes it unique should be added. A sermon, unlike a lecture, is presented in a context of worship. The very setting is different. It is presented in a sanctuary designed for the purpose of worship. Religious symbols remind people of the reality of the Christian faith. The sermon is a part of a service that includes religious music, the reading of the Scripture, the quietness and reverence of moments of silence and meditation—all of which have values in their own right and strengthen and support the sermon.

Worship creates a sense of community, of fellowship, of belonging—not only with our congregation but with all generations past, and with all believers everywhere. Dean Sperry of Harvard said that when he visited a European cathedral, it seemed inhabited by all the generations past and all the generations yet to come. That can be true in any service of worship.

Worship at its best is the highest expression of life—when we see reality in a new light, we become aware of grace and forgiveness, also of new possibilities for growth. We are challenged to new levels of life and a new willingness to serve.

All this doesn't happen in every service, but it could. To lead people in worship regularly week after week is one of the most significant tasks pastors can do.

From a pastoral point of view, nothing is as important as the pastoral prayer. George Buttrick once said that if a pastor has to choose between the prayer and the sermon, one had better forget the sermon. Fortunately no one has to make that choice.

In the pastoral prayer, the pastor expresses for the people praise, adoration, thanksgiving, confession, petition, aspiration, intercession, dedication, and commitment. What a privilege, and what a responsibility!

There are two approaches to this task. George Buttrick advocates preparing the prayer carefully, prayerfully, phrase-by-phrase, and word-by-word—more carefully than the sermon is prepared. This apparently was the method used by Fosdick in his classical book of pastoral prayers. Dr. Oren Baker, professor of pastoral counseling at Colgate-Rochester Divinity School, takes a different approach. He said that as he sat in the pulpit chair during the first part of the service, he studied the faces of the people—many that he had seen in his study. He tried to sense all their needs and hurts and hopes. Then when the time of prayer came, he tried to catch up their needs in a pastoral prayer.

Perhaps these two approaches are not mutually exclusive and can be blended wihout neglecting the values of either.

Here, then, is the one great hour for pastors. All the experiences of dealing with people one-by-one are in the background as pastors prepare and deliver the sermon. All their studies of Scripture, all their personal experiences, all their moments of prayer and meditation are combined as pastors link themselves with all the generations of great preachers who were also great pastors, as they speak to the people and lead them in prayer. What a tremendous challenge, and what a great opportunity!

# On Being a Pastor to Other Pastors

I was recently asked to speak to a group of pastors on the subject, "Who Cares for the Caretaker?" It is a good question.

One of the ironic facts of life is that the pastor has no pastor.

It is also true, in a sense, that the pastor's spouse has no pastor either.

The psychoanalyst has an analyst. Who ministers to the minister? Why not another pastor?

In anticipating this chapter, I thought of several statements of pastors. They represent several denominations and several communities. These are only one-sentence statements, so no one can possibly be identified, yet these statements are indicative of some of the kinds of concerns that pastors experience.

—I have to go to so many committee meetings that I don't have time to pray.

—Someone else always gets invited to make the big speeches at the conventions and serve on the important committees. I never do.

—One of my deacons is in insurance. He quit the ministry several years ago. He probably makes three times as much as I do.

—Let's face it, I'm a fraud.

—I didn't mean to get involved with that woman; it just happened.

—My wife and I just don't have much in common. If I stay married I'm not happy. If I get a divorce, I'll probably lose my church.

—I don't know why, but I'm just not committed as I ought to be.

—I would never advise any young person to go into the ministry.

—I'm mad at the church right now—nobody cares how hard you try.

There are similar statements of ministers' wives as well.

—I'm tired of being in second place. The church always comes first.

—He has plenty of time for other people and their problems but no time for us at home.

—It just isn't fair the way they treat my husband. All they do is gossip and complain.

—I'd like to take a nice vacation, go on a nice trip or something, but we can't afford it.

—When I met him, he was studying to be a doctor. I never wanted to be a minister's wife.

—I have a career too—now he has a chance to go to a better church in another town. What am I supposed to do? Give up all I've worked for and studied for? It isn't fair.

—I don't want to lead devotional services, go to all those boring women's meetings, and be a perfect house-keeper—maybe I'm just not cut out to be a minister's wife.

In more recent years, there have been some new developments due to the increase in the numbers of women in ministry. This is a very positive movement with much promise. In the future, there may be other subjects that need discussion, such as the pastor's husband and the complications that occur when both husband and wife are ordained. Do they serve the same church? Do they serve different churches? As yet, we do not have enough data to make any generalizations.

What do the statements listed previously say? They say that pastors are human, first of all, and like all other humans they get tired, anxious, discouraged, and upset. They have problems in their marriages and problems with their children, even as do doctors, lawyers, teachers, and everyone else.

Some of these emotional concerns, which are considered normal for other people, are accentuated for a pastor.

A pastor preaches on faith, is expected to be a person of faith, but the pastor also may experience doubt. Wasn't it Martin Luther, himself, who said, "Sometimes I believe and sometimes I doubt"?

Pastors usually have high expectations of themselves and of their performance. When they fall short, they feel guilty, often unnecessarily so. Guilt can be redemptive; it leads to repentance, commitment, and growth. Neurotic or unnecessary guilt can be a burden. It is a strange phenomenon that saints often feel more guilty than do sinners.

Pastors preach on love and forgiveness, but they often get frustrated and angry—then they feel guilty because they are angry. After all, aren't they supposed to love everybody? They also get discouraged, sometimes deeply discouraged. At such times, they need someone who can help.

Pastors often have very deep feelings of inadequacy. Part of these feelings simply is due to the fact that they are human, and as Alfred Adler said years ago, "To be human is to feel inadequate." Part of it is due to the nature of the vocation. Who is adequate for the ministry anyway?

We were told of an incident that occurred in an eastern seminary where George Buttrick was an annual guest. One year he spoke on preaching. He described it as the pastor's great responsibility; it took hours of preparation and great wisdom. The next year Buttrick came back and spoke on worship. He described the importance of worship, the pastor's role as leader of worship, and the great sigificance of the pastoral prayer. The third year he talked of pastoral care, the needs of persons one-by-one, sick persons, and troubled persons. This, he said, was the pastor's great responsibility. According to my friend's story, there was a student there who was a senior. He had heard all three presentations.

He said, "Dr. Buttrick, I have been here three years. Each year you have spoken of a different task. Each year you said that task was the most important thing we do, that it demands our full attention, that it takes hours of preparation—that's impossible."

Dr. Buttrick, without a moment's hesitation said, "You understand me perfectly. It's impossible, but that's what we're called to do."

As I said earlier, there is much emphasis in psychological circles these days on stress and tension.

I was asked to lead a group of pastors at a conference on "Stress in the Ministry." I began by listing five columns on the blackboard:

1. Stress Factors in Our Culture
2. Stress That Occurs in Our Economic and Vocational Life
3. Stress in Marriage and Family Life
4. Stress That Exists in Our National and International Life
5. Factors of Stress Unique to the Ministry

I then asked the pastors to fill in all the items of stress they could think of in the first four columns. We had a list of the usual things—inflation, competition, unemployment, problems with children and adolescents, noise, the media, the threat of atomic war—literally dozens and dozens of items. We soon filled the board and had to erase some to make room for others.

Then we came to the fifth column—Stress Factors in the Ministry. This was an equally impressive list. Some of the problems that were listed in the fifth column were: depending on volunteers, inadequate salary, burnout, the constant demand for creativity (one or more presentations a week), jealousy of other professions, competition between clergy, unrealistic expectations of the laity, living in a fishbowl, difficulty with authority figures (bishop, area minister, and others), the list went on and on. In fact, the list got so long, we cut off the discussion. We were feeling stress just thinking of all the stressful situations pastors face.

Most of the publications on stress and tension point out that there are some proven tension-reducing techniques that help reduce stress and are good antidotes to some of these pressures of our culture. Pastors tend to neglect these resources. For example:

1. Pastors tend to neglect their recreational life. When pastors say they haven't had a vacation in three years or a night home in six weeks, I suppose we are expected to be impressed, but an equally appropriate response is to think, "What are they trying to prove? Why do they assume they have to bring in the kingdom all by themselves?"

2. Pastors tend to neglect their intellectual growth. Their serious study stopped with the completion of seminary. As one pastor said, "I haven't read a serious book in six years; I don't have time." The result is that their preaching suffers; they feel angry at all they have to do and guilty for their own lack of growth.

3. Strange as it may seem, they neglect their own spiritual life. One pastor said, "I have let sermons on prayer become a substitute for praying."

Recognizing the importance of pastors building into their life-style some tension-reducing techniques, as valuable as these are, there are also times when pastors need personal guidance and counseling. On such occasions, pastors should do what they expect the members of the congregation to do—seek and accept help. Some pastors erroneously think that to accept help is a sign of weakness. This is not so. It is an act of personal maturity and a means whereby they can render a fuller, more effective ministry.

Having said all this, let's point out that pastors, in the main, make good counselees. (1) They are highly motivated to change. They believe in the possibility of change or they wouldn't be in the ministry. (2) They are highly verbal, and counseling and psychotherapy, by definition, are forms of verbal healing. (3) They have good communication skills, and again, counseling is mainly communication. (4) They (usually) are of a high level of intelligence (at least most are college graduates), which means they can come to insights quickly. (5) They understand the counseling process. This is especially true of those who have had good training in counseling. They understand both the counselor's role and their own. (6) Pastors are receptive to religious practices and spiritual resources such as prayer and meditation—a strange world to many secular counselees and counselors.

It is occasionally (even frequently in some cases) the pastor's privilege and responsibility to counsel another minister. A pastor has two unique qualifications for such a service. (1) The clergy tends to verbalize their concerns in theological language, with biblical illustrations. (2) Many of their problems are church-related. Another pastor who is familiar with such terminology and who knows the problems of the church is in a position to offer helpful guidance and counsel.

There may be occasions when a pastor feels obligated to decline counseling another pastor. If the two are close friends and the pastor feels it would be difficult to remain objective, it would be better to suggest another pastor as counselor. If the pastor feels the problems described indicate the need of a physician, psychologist, or psychiatrist, the pastor must say so. In either case, the pastor can maintain friendship, which itself can be very therapeutic.

It is always a challenge to work with another pastor because such work has such far-reaching implications. There is the need of the pastor first of all, which is the primary concern. There is the benefit that the counseling will bring to the pastor's family as well. There is also the fact that by helping the pastor, we indirectly help all the persons to whom the pastor will minister more effectively, and thus in a very real sense, we help the church as a whole.

# THIRTEEN

# Helping People Relax and Have Fun

Helping people have fun is a legitimate ministry. Life is serious enough. Anything that will help people relax, let down, laugh, smile, enjoy, is a real service.

Having fun is also an excellent antidote for the anxieties and frustrations we deal with in counseling and psychotherapy. I have long felt that what we do in traditional counseling is too limited. For example, even in extended counseling we usually see a person only one hour a week. That means there are one hundred sixty-seven hours before that person comes in again. What do people do during that time to reduce tension, relieve strain, or to find some pleasure and satisfaction in their lives?

It is true that some problems can be resolved by direct attack. We discuss the problem frankly and honestly; we try to gain insight into its origin and hopefully come to its resolution. However, there are some problems that can be greatly alleviated and some that can be actually solved by cultivating resources or a way of life that is incompatible with the problem.

Relaxation is the classic example. You can't be tense and relaxed at the same time. That is a truism. Every emotion has a physiological accompaniment. The accompaniment of anxiety is tension. Tension and relaxation are incompatible. Therefore, in training people to relax we reduce the tension. The physician who pioneered in this field was Edmund Jacobsen of the University of Chicago. He took patients into his laboratory, trained them to relax by focusing their attention on different muscle groups, starting with the right arm. He had the patient practice relaxing the arm for one hour a day for a week. Then he moved to the left arm and progressed through all the muscles of the body. This process took several weeks, but it had surprising results. He found he was not only curing some physical ills but was reducing anxiety as well, without ever talking about the things that made them anxious. He published his findings in two books: one for doctors called *Progressive Relaxation* and one for laypersons called *You Must Relax* (McGraw-Hill, 1957).

Josef Wolpe, a psychiatrist trained in the analytic tradition, read these books and tried relaxation training with his patients. He found he could simplify the procedure by training his patients to relax in one session and then having them practice relaxation between sessions. He, too, was pleased with the results.

None of this is really new. There is an ancient proverb that says, "You will break the bow if you keep it always stretched." That originated when bows and arrows were the means of securing food and protecting life. The principle is as true today as it was then—many people are stretched to the breaking point. They need something to reduce the tension. In other words, "They who never let go can't hang on."

Some people are so tense they need special training such as Jacobsen or Wolpe gave. (My experience is that Wolpe's method of training them in one session is sufficient.) They have learned to be tense by a multitude of repetitions until it is almost automatic. They need to be trained to relax so that it, too, will be automatic.

Relaxation reduces tension, increases efficiency, improves performance in everything from golf to public speaking. God gave us the power to work and to strive. He also gave us the power to rest and relax.

Several years ago Richard Cabot, that unique physician who made such a contribution to the ministry in the early days of the pastoral care movement, wrote a book entitled *What Men Live By.* Today he would no doubt call it *What People Live By,* but this was before we were so careful about sexist language. There was nothing sexist about the contents, however. In the introduction, Dr. Cabot pointed out that he wrote it with persons in mind who were sick but with no physical illness. It was his thesis that there are four great areas that give life value. These were:

### Work—Play—Love—Worship

Society tells us we have to work, and elsewhere in these pages, I note the value of work. Psychologists, preachers, marriage counselors tell us we need to love. I found it interesting that a physician wrote of the value of worship.

What impressed me as being unique about the book was his listing play as one of the four things we live by.

Everyone needs something to do just for the fun of it. It has been said that a Puritan is one who is afraid there is someone somewhere who is having a good time. We need to have a good time because having a good time is healthy.

Again, we must keep it all in perspective. The New Testament does not say, "Seek first pleasure . . . " it says, "Seek first the kingdom . . . ," which means live a life of service. But we will serve better, do our work more effectively, if we also have some fun along the way.

It doesn't matter all that much what we do for fun, as long as we enjoy it. Horace Bushnell liked to fish; Winston Churchill liked to paint; Jerry Ford likes to play golf; Norman Cousins likes to play the organ; and Rosey Grier likes to needlepoint. He even wrote a book about it—and I for one wouldn't argue his right.

Recreation should be fun. There are too many people who make work out of their recreation. It is simply work for which they don't get paid.

There is an added value if our recreation is done out-of-doors. There is a healing power in nature that those of us who live in concrete canyons miss. More of this in a moment.

There is a real value in play. As technology increases and the work-week decreases, a creative use of leisure becomes more and more important. It well may be that avocational guidance will be as important in the future as vocational guidance is now.

Finding time to enjoy the out-of-doors has several values. It is healthy, for one thing, but equally important, there is a real value in being aware of the beauty of nature.

There is an interesting story in the life of Alice Freeman Palmer, which tells of her work with children in the slums of Boston. One day one of the children said, "Tell us how to be happy." Alice Palmer was taken aback for a moment for she knew the squalid conditions in which the children lived. In a moment of inspiration she said, "Okay, I will give you three rules which, if you follow every day, you will be happy." The three rules were:

1. See something beautiful every day.
2. Learn something new every day.
3. Do something for someone else every day.

Even though finding things of beauty in the slums wasn't easy, one child discovered a geranium in a window box. Another said because it rained and she had to stay indoors, she saw a sparrow taking a bath in the gutter and that was beautiful.

Alice Palmer gave them a method for counteracting the drab surroundings in which they lived and helped them be aware of the beautiful, even in unlikely places.

I mentioned the value of rest and relaxation in reducing tension. The opposite is also true—physical activity reduces tension also, fosters sleep, diminishes anxiety, improves our health.

Will Durant the philosopher says we go against nature when we fail to get regular exercise. He contends that it was never intended that we use only our minds and not our bodies; yet thousands of people ride to and from the office, sit at a desk all day, ride home, and sit in front of a television set all evening. He contends that everyone should have at least an hour's physical exercise every day.

Our bodies were meant to be used, yet by and large, we don't use them. Few of us get fifteen minutes' exercise a day let alone Durant's recommendation of one hour. This would have been a foolish recommendation a few generations ago. We were then an agricultural people who mostly lived on farms. We did our own chores, raised our own vegetables, churned our own butter. When we wanted to go someplace, we rode a horse or walked. When evening came we were too tired to be anxious. We went to sleep to get enough rest for the plowing we had to do the next day.

There are some whose jobs require physical activity today. For them this section is inappropriate. They need other forms of respite. As someone has said, "When the body is tired, exercise the mind. When the mind is tired, exercise the body."

Our need for exercise is recognized by specialists in both physical fitness and mental health. There are opportunities enough. Newspapers are filled with advertisements for health clubs, spas, exercise programs. Actually, we don't need to invest a lot of money in an exercise program—a good pair of walking shoes is all we need. In fact, brisk walking—I prefer the word *striding*—is as good as any exercise.

Whatever we choose—a health club, jogging, swimming, calisthenics—it should be done under the guidance of a physician if there is any physical reason we should be careful. We need to work into it gradually, so there is no strain involved. It it important that exercise be done regularly. Occasional bursts of exercise have no lasting value and may even be harmful.

I have found myself more and more recommending that my counselees participate in an exercise program between sessions. I recall one woman who was very discouraged to the point of being almost inactive. I recommended that she get out of the house (the healing power of nature) and walk briskly (the restoring power of activity) for fifteen minutes morning and evening. I am not so naive as to think that this resolved all her difficulties, but it did get the breeze in her face, enabled her to hear the birds sing, got her blood circulating, helped her sleep better—who knows, maybe it did more good than my counseling sessions.

Of all the tension-reducing techniques, none is more valuable than humor. No one has given more eloquent testimony to this than Norman Cousins in his book *The Anatomy of an Illness.* Those who know his story know that he made a conscious effort to cultivate humor as a means of overcoming his illness. There is no question in his mind as to its effectiveness.

Humor has been defined as the ability *not* to take ourselves too seriously. Gordon Allport, in one of his books, said something to the effect that when patients can laugh at themselves, the neurosis is broken.

Humor, like an awareness of the beautiful, must be cultivated.

I am well aware that humor can be cruel, even sick. Humor that hurts, embarrasses, or degrades anyone is not healthy. Also, as a total philosophy, it is inadequate. We have all seen people try to go wisecracking through life—that is unhealthy—even unchristian.

The word *humor* never appears in the Bible, although it does say that God laughed, and well he might when you consider what we, his children, sometimes do. You have to have a sense of humor to describe a man blowing on a trumpet so everyone will see what he puts in the collection plate, or someone choking on a gnat but swallowing a whole camel.

Humor is the great tension-reducer. It unifies a group, reduces tension, helps keep things in perspective.

All this depends on developing certain attitudes—the kind of attitudes described by Clyde Reid in *Celebrate the Temporary* (Harper & Row, 1972), a useful book for the pastor to have in the church's library. Reid doesn't pretend problems don't exist. He recognizes that there is pain, bills to pay and problems to be solved, but he stresses the fact that there are also people to be enjoyed, beauty to be appreciated, pleasure to be experienced—here and now.

This chapter has not dealt with ultimates. It has dealt with secondary things—relaxation, rest, play, beauty, and humor—but they are great possessions. The pastor who can help people appreciate them and enjoy them has performed a real ministry—one that is often overlooked.

# · F O U R T E E N ·

# To Meet the Challenge

I trust that anyone who has read this far recognizes the fact that parish pastoral counseling presents both a challenge and great opportunities. I also trust that any who have read this far have asked themselves such questions as, "Who is adequate for such tasks?" "How can I improve?" "How can I do it better?"

I will list ten suggestions that will help a parish pastor render a larger service. Not all apply to every pastor. Probably all pastors are already doing some of these things. Probably no pastor is doing all of them as well as he or she might. There may be others, but these are important.

## 1. Prepare thoroughly.

The ministry is a profession in the best sense of the word. All professions make great demands upon their candidates and members. This is as it should be. The parish pastor should be thoroughly trained—biblically, theologically, and historically. The pastor must also be trained in the performance of pastoral skills—homiletical, educational, and administrative. If the pastor is to assume the great responsibilities of working with people and their deepest concerns (and no pastor can really avoid this), then the pastor must also be trained in understanding human behavior and on counseling procedures.

### 2. Be a lifelong student.

A seminary education is a good place to start. If we are to meet the challenge of parish pastoral counseling, however, we must recognize that seminary education is only the beginning. This is a lifelong task. Other professionals who work with people read professional journals, attend workshops and seminars, return to school for refresher courses, are participating in some form of continuing education. As one man put it, "Dedicated ignorance is still ignorance." Continued study is needed not only because there are new developments every year, but because we need to be in a constant program of growth to meet the increasing demands that come with added experience.

### 3. Find a good consultant.

Perhaps the most important thing we have learned from the Clinical Pastoral Education movement is the value of supervision and consultation. Any pastor who does extensive counseling would benefit from regular sessions with a qualified consultant. It may be another pastor trained in supervisory procedures, a hospital chaplain, or a psychologist and psychiatrist who understand the nature of the church and ministry. Regular consultation has many values. It helps the pastor understand the dynamics of what is taking place; it helps the pastor evaluate the effectiveness of his or her methods and procedures; it helps the pastor to understand the emotional involvement that may be taking place between pastor and parishioner, and at times becomes very therapeutic for the pastor as well.

### 4. Establish your own priorities.

The Parish pastor has so many varied responsibilities and there are so many demands upon the pastor's time and energy that unless he or she has certain priorities, the things that really matter will get crowded out by things that do not matter much. I am deeply convinced that human need is the top priority on a pastor's time. This does not dismiss or minimize the importance of many other activities such as study, administration, or recreation. I shall speak of their value in this list. It does mean, however, that the pastor must be very clear about his or her priorities and then schedule time accordingly.

### 5. Evaluate, schedule, and control your time.

Pastoral counseling and pastoral care take time. Some things can be done in a hurry, but not good counseling. Sermon preparation, church administration, to say nothing of recreation and family life, all take time also. If human need is high on the pastor's priority list, if the pastor sees working with individuals as being as important as we claim it is, and if he or she is to meet these challenges and fulfill the other responsibilities as well, there is only one solution—a careful and prayerful evaluation and management of time.

This has other values as well. We know from working with many pastors that those who make a careful and prayerful evaluation of their time often find they have more time available than they realized and have discovered one of the best means to reduce stress and strain.

### 6. Cultivate the capacity to concentrate.

This follows directly on the subject of time. We not only need to learn to schedule time, but to do one thing at a time—this means concentration. Timothy Galwey, talking about tennis, says that concentration is the finest of the fine arts because all other arts depend on it. That is true. Whether it is a concert pianist, a surgeon, a scholar in the library, a professional golfer, or a parish pastoral counselor—their effectiveness depends on concentration. Concentration consists of two functions—"shutting out" and "focusing down." We must shut out all distractions, all concerns of yesterday or tomorrow, and focus on the task at hand. To a golfer, this means that he or she must shut out the distractions of the crowd, the opponent's score, the presence of the TV cameras, the size of the purse, and focus on this shot and this shot alone. For the parish pastoral counselor, this means that he or she must shut out all other matters about the church, all personal concerns, and focus down on this person and this person only. It was said of Phillips Brooks that when he had someone in his study, no matter how many others were waiting, no matter whether his next Sunday's sermon was prepared or not, that person felt that his problem was all that Brooks had on his mind. Phillips Brooks never had a course in pastoral counseling but he was a good pastoral counselor because he could concentrate so well.

### 7. Use the services of other professionals.

We would not respect a doctor who didn't make a referral when a specialist was indicated. The parish pastoral counselor needs to recognize his or her own limitations. In an earlier chapter, I mentioned the great value that the presence of other specialists—both pastoral and psychological—can have for the pastor. Whenever the pastor does not have the time to deal with a situation thoroughly and responsibly, the pastor should help the person find someone who can. When the pastor does not have the training or the resources to meet a person's particular needs, he or she should do the same. There are occasions when a pastor's relationship with a parishioner may be such that the pastor feels some other pastor or a specialist could be more objective. In many of these situations the pastor may continue in a pastoral role while a specialist assumes the treatment responsibilities. In other words, the pastor is familiar with and uses all the resources of the community for the good of his or her parishioners.

### 8. Find time for rest, relaxation, and recreation.

At a busy time in Jesus' ministry, he said to the disciples, "Come away by yourselves to a lonely place, and rest a while" (Mark 6:31). It is true, as some of my friends have pointed out when I have quoted this verse, that when they got to the other side of the lake, a crowd had anticipated them and was waiting for them, and Jesus ministered to them. The fact remains that those who assume heavy responsibilities need to find time to lay them down—to relax and rest. After all, according to Genesis, even God rested one day out of seven. As an old preacher of limited formal training but great practical wisdom put it, "Don't try to stomp out sin before sundown." It is not withdrawal in order to escape responsibility that I advocate—it is withdrawal for rest and renewal in order that we can return and accept greater responsibility and render a larger service.

### 9. Spend much time in prayer.

Perhaps it is unnecessary to include this in a list intended for the clergy—however, the list would be incomplete without it. The prayer of which I speak is of two kinds. There are the prayers we offer for ourselves, that we will have patience and understanding, that we will have the capacity to relate, to communicate, and to care. The others are the prayers we offer for those with whom we counsel. I am not going to debate the efficacy of intercessory prayer except to say that the great pastors believed in it.

When John Frederic Oberlin was carrying on his great ministry in the Vasges mountains of France, he kept a notebook in which he listed the names and needs of his people. He would spend an hour a day praying for his people by name. The people would pass his house in silence during that hour. They knew he was praying for them. No wonder he was a great pastor. Great pastors have usually been great intercessors.

### 10. Deepen your sense of trust.

Eric Erikson, the noted psychologist, said that if he were asked to state the first component of mental health, it would be a "basic trust." In other words the first component of parish pastoral counseling is a basic trust. It is a trust in ourselves and our ability to understand and communicate. It is a trust in others and their capacity to grow—to change, to mature, to come to insights. It is a trust in the methods we use and in the value of the counseling process. Underneath it all is a trust in God, that God cares more about these persons than we do, that God is present whenever two people honestly, humbly, sincerely face the deeper issues of life.

Faithfully applying these ten suggestions will help the pastor meet the challenge and realize the great opportunities of pastoral counseling in the parish setting.

# · F I F T E E N ·

# Conclusion: The Wounded Healers

The first sentence of Arthur McGiffert's *Life of Martin Luther* says, "Great men need not that we praise them; the need is ours that we know them." One of the greatest sources for understanding life and its meaning is a study of the lives of great men and women, especially those whose lives have been given in service to others. They remind us what life can be.

Just to meet in a book people such as Abraham Lincoln, Ralph Waldo Emerson, Marie Curie, Clara Barton, Mahatma Gandhi, Louis Pasteur, or John Milton is an inspiration. Granted they are all "five-talent" people, while we may have but two talents or even only one, but the same principles that applied in their lives apply in ours. The same resources that were available to them are available to us.

In terms of the subjects discussed in this study, our

greatest interest is in the lives of great pastors and psychologists, primarily psychotherapists. In reflecting on their lives, one thing stands out—they all had one thing in common. Every one of them experienced some form of difficulty, some pain, some frustration. That was true of all the persons listed above. It was true of Martin Luther, John Wesley, Horace Bushnell, Phillips Brooks, Washington Gladden, and Harry Emerson Fosdick. It was true of all great preachers and religious leaders. It was equally true of William James, Sigmund Freud, Alfred Adler, Carl Jung, and Carl Rogers—all great psychologists. The true healers of the mind and spirit have gained their skill and sensitivity, at least in part, through personal struggle.

Henri J. M. Nouwen wrote a book entitled *The Wounded Healer*. Speaking of the minister, Nouwen said, "He is called to be the wounded healer, the one who must look after his own wounds but at the same time be prepared to heal the wounds of others" (Doubleday & Co., 1979, p. 82).

In Thornton Wilder's play *The Angel That Troubled the Waters* is a scene by a pool, where according to tradition, an angel comes periodically and stirs the waters. The first person in the water after this occurs will be healed.

Naturally, the pool is surrounded by people, all wishing to be healed. Among them is a physician who is himself suffering from a sickness but is able to work. As he works, he silently prays that the angel might trouble the waters while he is there so he might be healed.

The angel does appear, but refuses his request and asks him where his power would be without his wound. The angel also reminds him that it is his remorse that makes his "voice tremble into the affairs of men. The very angels themselves cannot persuade the wretched and blundering children on earth as can one human being broken on the wheels of living. In Love's service only the wounded soldier can serve" (Coward-McCann, 1928, p. 149).

The great men of Scripture knew this experience also. Moses felt so insecure that he had to seek Aaron's help because he couldn't speak (Exod. 3:11). Jeremiah felt inadequate for his call and tried to avoid it (Jer. 1:6). Simon Peter, after making great boasts of his loyalty and obedience, fell far short, even denying any relationship to Jesus before the questioning of a temple maid. He knew of his failure and wept bitterly. And of course Paul apparently experienced some sort of handicap that troubled him greatly. Scholars have offered various suggestions as to what it was, but no one really knows. Paul called it a "thorn . . . in the flesh," which could mean anything. "Three times I besought the Lord about this, that it should leave me; but he said to me, 'My grace is sufficient for you, for my power is made perfect in weakness'" (II Cor. 12:7-9).

As for Jesus, his whole story is centered in a cross.

This has been true historically. The great healers of mind and spirit have usually been those who knew the pain of their own wounds.

William James was said to be such a dynamic, courageous personality that he inspired others by his very presence. Yet he went through a period of deep discouragement and said his reason for studying psychology was "to find a balm for the soul."

Phillips Brooks was a noted preacher and a magnetic personality. When William James was asked to define *spiritual*, he said he couldn't do it, but he knew a spiritual man when he saw one, and that was Phillips Brooks. Yet Phillips Brooks at one time felt so inadequate that he refused to see his friends.

Horace Bushnell is referred to as the preacher's preacher. His sermon "Every Man's Life a Plan of God" is said to be one of the three greatest sermons in the English language. Yet he said, "I know what it is to have the purest motives, most fervent prayers, and most incessant labors misapprehended and misrepresented" (Mary A. Cheney, *Life and Letters of Horace Bushnell,* Scribner, 1903, p. 518).

Washington Gladden was a great preacher, lecturer, and writer. His books and sermons brought faith and hope to thousands. He is best known as the author of the hymn, "O Master, Let Me Walk with Thee." It was surprising to discover that one who could write such a statement of faith spent years of struggle and perplexity, desperately trying to find some assurance of what he called the "favor of God."

These people not only knew such experiences, but they actually grew by them. A professor of mine used to say, "It is out of our greatest difficulties that our greatest insights come."

There is no course in any seminary catalog, to my knowledge, on how to deal with difficulty and discouragement, but it may well be a determining factor in their graduates' usefulness and effectiveness. I will not go so far as to say you can't be a good pastor without it, but you are somewhat at a disadvantage unless you have experienced it.

I once made a rather thorough study of homiletic literature. The sermon that impressed me most was Harry Emerson Fosdick's "Handicapped Lives." In this sermon he said, "The great work of the world has been done by handicapped people." That may be an exaggeration, but there's truth in it.

Fosdick used many illustrations from his vast knowledge of biography. He referred to Louis Pasteur who was partially paralyzed at forty-six, Henry M. Stanley who was born in a poor house, Beethoven who was deaf and could not hear his own compositions, and Milton who was blind but wrote a sonnet on his own blindness.

We can add many others. Abraham Lincoln never had more than three months' schooling in his life. Denied schooling, he would not be denied an education. His speeches are read by every school child in America. No statesman ever spoke greater words than those of his second inaugural address, "With malice toward none, with charity for all. With firmness in the right as God gives us to see the right. . . ."

There are Franklin D. Roosevelt, a victim of polio; George Mathieson, the blind hymn writer; and of course Helen Keller, who could not see, hear, or speak but who not only demonstrated great courage but made great contributions to other handicapped people (Fosdick, "Handicapped Lives" in *The Power to See It Through,* Harper & Brothers, 1935).

There is another proverb, from Arabia: "Because I have been athirst, I will dig a well, that others may drink."

Fosdick himself is a case in point. Early in his career he wrote a little book, now becoming a devotional classic, *The Meaning of Prayer.* Late in his ministry, when asked why he wrote the book, he said that it came out of young manhood's struggle. "I desperately needed something to hang onto."

Charles Dickens was born in poverty. His father was thrown into a debtor's prison. As a boy, Dickens cried himself to sleep at night out of hunger and embarrassment, but the people he knew in the London slums became characters in his novels, and he did as much to arouse the conscience of the English people as all the reformers combined.

You say Dickens and Fosdick were people of great brilliance, and I agree. They were five-talent people whereas we have only two or one. But the same principle applies to us as well.

Because they had been athirst they chose "to dig a well that others might drink." This is what Alfred Adler called turning a minus into a plus.

I'm not saying we should seek trouble or look for pain. Far from it. We don't want a martyr complex. Pastors spend most of their professional lives helping people evade, avoid, or rise above trouble.

No one escapes it entirely. The biblical record is quite clear at this point, taking trouble for granted. The Bible says trouble not only can be overcome, but it can be transcended.

Henry Churchill King used to point out that the great sources of our religious life, with its appropriate emotional response, are not introspective exercises, but sharing in the insights and experiences of others. In fact, King felt that there were no lessons in life that were more important than the lessons we could learn by comparing our lives with the lives of "far greater souls" (King, *The Laws of Friendship Human and Divine*, Macmillan, 1916, p. 132).

Now we are back to the same place we started from in the first chapter. The pastoral ministry is a great heritage. To be a part of that tradition is a great privilege. The world is full of troubled, needy people—people who can be helped by one who cares, one who serves in the name of him who cared most of all.

# Appendix: Fifty Years of Pastoral Counseling

At the suggestion of my publisher, I am including an appendix that summarizes some of my experiences of pastoral counseling, particularly pastoral counseling in a local church setting. It was my editor's feeling that some readers might be interested in knowing something of the background out of which these ideas came.

I was licensed to preach in 1934 and ordained to the ministry in 1935 and have been engaged in some form of pastoral counseling ever since. I attended Drake University, a church-related institution where, strange as it may sound, I was a math major. My original ambition was to teach mathematics and combine that with a coaching career. I had the traditional courses in undergraduate psychology but recall very little about them except that they aroused no great interest in human need or any thought of pursuing a career either in the pastorate or counseling. As I continued work on my B. A. degree, my interests shifted from mathematics to religion and from the school to the church. However, in order to pursue a theological degree, I had to make up some deficiencies before I could be admitted into graduate study for the ministry. My only regret is that I did not spend more time in social studies, especially sociology and psychology, for they would have given me a better background for my later training.

I did enroll in the divinity school of Drake University and accepted a position in the University Christian Church where my major responsibilities were with the high school and university students. I anticipated that my primary concerns would center around programming for young people but soon found that high school and college students had many problems I had not even dreamed about. My studies in the seminary gave me a deep appreciation of the Scriptures and the historic tradition of the church, but gave me almost no help in dealing with the problems that the young people were presenting in my office.

I was well aware that I needed more practical training if I were to fulfill the kind of responsibilities I was being confronted with, so I enrolled in Colgate-Rochester Divinity School, which had a reputation for preparing pastors for a practical ministry. Here we did have one course in pastoral counseling, taught by Oren Baker. He had been a successful pastor and had taken his Ph.D. degree at the University of Chicago with a major emphasis in psycho-therapy. This course was an inspiration to me, although we had few materials to work with by today's standards. Our bibliography then had only a few books on pastoral counseling and pastoral care, and a few on general counseling and psychotherapy. Today there are hundreds of books on pastoral care and counseling and even more on counseling, guidance, and psychotherapy.

While I was pursuing this degree I served as an assistant pastor at the Grace Methodist Church of Rochester, where I was responsible for the young adults. I soon found that young adults, as well as students, had problems. Graduation from college only changed the nature of some of the problems.

After I had completed my seminary training, I accepted the call to a church of about five hundred members in a small town in upstate New York. I can still recall one Sunday morning as I sat in the chancel of the church and surveyed the people who had come that morning to worship. It was not a large crowd and I had not been there a very long time, but it had been long enough for me to know the concerns of some of the people who were assembled there. On the back row was a young man who was there for only one reason. The police said he had to be. He had been involved in a series of delinquencies and misdemeanors, and part of the condition on which he could stay out of jail was to be in church each Sunday morning. Close to the front was a young couple who was there because we had had a funeral service for their infant child that week. On the right-hand aisle was a high school teacher who had one of the most brilliant minds I had ever encountered. She had been to see me that week to discuss her religious faith. She didn't know what she believed, or if she believed in anything at all. A woman in the choir that morning was very pale. She hadn't been getting much sleep because she didn't know whether to try to continue an intolerable marriage relationship. I can remember it as if it were yesterday. I can also remember the feeling of helplessness and inadequacy that swept over me as I pondered what to say to these people that would really be of help, and even more important, how could I help them when they came to see me in the church study?

Because of these feelings I felt the need of more training so I enrolled in the extension department of the graduate school of the University of Chicago and took an extension course under Charles Holman, one of the pioneers in the pastoral counseling movement. One of my assignments was to write a paper comparing the work of the modern pastor with the work of pastors of a previous generation. I found there was no information on the history of pastoral work. There were histories of doctrine, histories of preaching, histories of religious education but no histories of pastoral care. I dropped the course and began to collect material. It took me seven years but I ended up writing a history of pastoral care entitled *Physicians of the Soul*.

However, before I finished the manuscript I received a call to a church in the Midwest. Here my experience was the same as it had been everywhere else. A major portion of my time was being taken by people who were troubled, some of them deeply troubled, with every problem I could imagine and some I had not even known existed.

After ten years of experience in these two churches, I felt there was only one solution and that was to seek continued training. There were no seminaries offering doctorates in pastoral care then as there are today, so I was forced to go to the state universities. I had no desire to leave the ministry and become a secular counselor, and I soon found that there were not many graduate programs available to a graduate student who wanted to stay in the pastorate. The University of Nebraska, however, was an exception. They took the position that they could give me good training in counseling and they didn't care where I used it—the YMCA, a social agency, a school, or the church. I was especially fortunate in securing as my major professor Dean A. Worcester, who himself had at one time considered the ministry and knew exactly what I wanted to do. In fact, when I proposed that I do my thesis in counseling psychology just to test myself at that level, Dr. Worcester insisted that I should do it in my own field of interest, which was the church. I chose as my topic "The Religious Counseling of College Students," which later was published under the title *Counseling University Students*.

In order to feed my family I served as the executive secretary of the university YMCA and once again found myself counseling with college students. At the same time I was serving on Sundays as the chaplain of the state reformatory so found myself working with young men from vastly different areas of experience.

When I finished my degree I became the senior minister of the First Christian Church of Lincoln, Nebraska. It was a downtown church and also close to the university campus. Here I found myself exposed to a wide range of human problems—much more than I had experienced in my previous pastorates, both of which were with much smaller congregations. I divided my days, spending my mornings in sermon preparation and writing and my afternoons in counseling and pastoral care. My studies at the university had made me aware of some blind spots in the pastoral care literature, so I did some writing in such areas as the gifted, the retarded, vocational choice, always as it related to the pastorate.

After six years I received a call to serve on the faculty of Brite Divinity School, the graduate seminary of Texas Christian University. I resisted the call for a long time because I was happy where I was. I enjoyed the parish, I enjoyed the church I had, and I was not at all sure I could teach at the graduate level. Finally I was convinced that I had a responsibility to help train pastors for the church. It was really out of a sense of obligation that I accepted. It did seem to me that the greatest contribution I could make to the church was to help train pastors in what I had come to believe was one of the most sacred areas of the pastoral task—pastoral care and counseling. I became a part of the graduate faculty, feeling very much like a misplaced pastor in the midst of scholars.

I shall never forget the first day I met my classes. After making thorough preparation, at the end of the day I went to the dean's office and said I had a problem. I had taught them everything I knew, and there were fifteen more weeks to go in the semester.

However, I stayed for twenty-one years and thoroughly enjoyed the experience. Prior to my class, there had been only one course in pastoral theology covering everything of a practical nature that a pastor can be called upon to do. This included weddings, funerals, fund raising, baptisms, and calling on the sick. We developed a department that dealt with pastoral care exclusively. It was an exciting time. An outline of my basic introductory course, *Learning About Pastoral Care,* was published by Abingdon Press. It was during this time that most of my counseling was done with seminary students and their wives or spouses, plus many laypersons referred to me by local pastors.

This was also during the time the Clinical Pastoral Education movement was making a real contribution to theological education. We started our own Pastoral Care and Training Center and used advanced, carefully selected students as counselors. This meant that I added the responsibility of supervision to my lectures and seminars. It also meant that I saw the needs of literally hundreds of persons through the experiences of the student interns I was supervising. In supervising students I tried to help them focus on four different areas. One was the dynamics that were taking place in the lives of their counselees. Two was the methods they were using. Were they effective or not? Three was the relationship that existed between them and their counselees. And, finally, what were the theological implications of what they were doing? The weekly seminars that we conducted with our staff were also published by Abingdon Press in *A Pastoral Counseling Guidebook.*

Five days after my retirement from the faculty of the seminary, at the invitation of Dr. Albert Pennybacker, I came across the street to the University Christian Church where I serve as the consultant in pastoral counseling. Now, to an even larger extent, I am doing the things I had been teaching and writing about. Throughout all of this, I try to keep abreast of the literature on both pastoral counseling and general psychotherapy. I also try to maintain my own effectiveness by continued consultation with people who are especially qualified to evaluate my work. At the present time I have regular sessions with Kenneth Timken, who was at one time a Presbyterian pastor, then a chaplain in a mental hospital, and is now a practicing psychiatrist. He knows exactly what I am trying to do and our sessions together have been the best form of continuing education I can imagine.

As I reflect back on these experiences, I have no idea how many books I have read or how many people I have counseled—it would run into the thousands in both cases. I wish I had kept a record, but it is probably just as well that I didn't because I doubt if people would believe me anyway.

It does seem to me that there are a few general principles that stand out.

First is the fact that the world is full of troubled people. This is ubiquitous. They are everywhere: in every town, in every community, in every congregation. They need help.

My second observation is that everyone has problems of some kind or another, at some time or other. This is not to say that all people are maladjusted or neurotic. It is simply to recognize that life being what it is, sooner or later all people experience disappointment, anxiety, feelings of inadequacy, or guilt. It is true in the biblical record. It is obvious to anyone who studies biography. It should be evident to any pastor.

Third, I have become convinced, at times amazed at the power of the human spirit to transcend pain and difficulty and to attain higher levels of courage and faith. This is true not only in the biographies of the saints, but it is true of a lot of common people in every congregation in America. I consider it both a privilege and an inspiration to have worked with large numbers of these people.

Fourth, I am convinced that one of the most sacred tasks a pastor has to perform is to minister to members of the congregation or the community, one by one. This is not to minimize preaching, teaching, or administration. These, too, are sacred responsibilities. But I believe that human need should have first priority over a pastor's time and that both preaching and administration should be person-minded and will be done more effectively if they are.

Finally, I am convinced that the local pastor is in a key position to render a great, if not the greatest, service to anyone in the community. I have been associated with many pastors over the years, some as students, some as friends, some as counselees. They are a fine group of people and deserve all the encouragement and support they can receive both from denominational officials and laypersons in the church.

Pastoral counseling as a part of a minister's responsibilities is both old and new. It is as old as the biblical record; it is as new as the latest book reviewed in the *Journal of Pastoral Care*. When I consider the progress that has been made over the last five decades, the results are remarkable. We have resources that no previous generation of pastors had at all. We have understandings now that I knew nothing about when I served the churches mentioned earlier. When we consider the vast needs, the number of people who need to be helped, the areas we still do not understand, we realize that there is much left to be done. There is much to be grateful for, and the future of pastoral counseling in a local church setting is very promising. It is truly a great challenge and a tremendous opportunity.